MATT MORAN is head chef and co-owner of ARIA restaurant, which enjoys one of the most enviable reputations and locations in the city, overlooking the Sydney Opera House and harbour. In 2009 he opened a second ARIA restaurant in Brisbane, also in a stunning waterfront location on Eagle Street Pier. As an industry icon, Matt has featured in a number of television series, including *My Restaurant Rules*, *The Heat in the Kitchen* and *The Chopping Block*, and is a judge on Network Ten's top-rating series *MasterChef Australia*.

He is the author of two bestselling cookbooks also published by Lantern, *Matt Moran* and *When I Get Home*.

DINNER AT MATT'S

MATT MORAN

PHOTOGRAPHY BY CHRIS CHEN

LANTERN
an imprint of
PENGUIN BOOKS

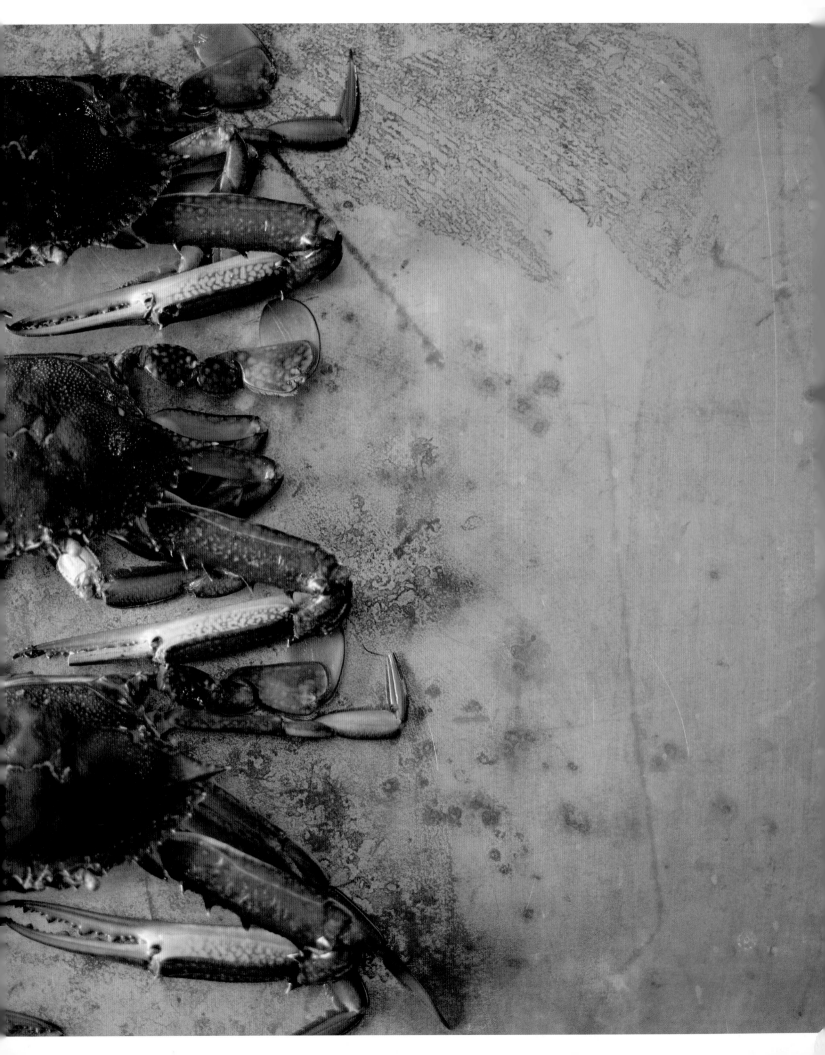

INTRODUCTION

There is nothing I love more than having friends and family over for a meal. I enjoy the whole process – planning the menu, visiting my favourite provedores and markets in search of the best seasonal produce, settling down in the kitchen to cook, matching wines to the food and, finally, welcoming my guests and enjoying their company. I find it relaxing and therapeutic cooking in my kitchen at home – quite different to cooking in the restaurant kitchen – so for me it doesn't get much better.

There are two kinds of dinner party, both equally rewarding. Those where you do a lot of forward planning and set aside plenty of time for the cooking, and those spur-of-the-moment occasions where you need to whip something up in a hurry. There are recipes in this book to suit both of these occasions – when you want to spoil your guests with lovingly prepared dishes that are as good as anything they might eat in a restaurant, or those times when you want a simple recipe that you can throw together without too much fuss.

What you decide to cook will depend on many factors – the season, your guests, the occasion – so I have tried to include a broad selection of starters, seafood, poultry, meat and vegetarian dishes and, of course, some delicious desserts. To help you choose what dishes to serve together, there is a selection of suggested menus that I hope will tempt and inspire you. On a warm summer's night you might go for a summer barbecue, or perhaps a Mediterranean-style dinner. In the heart of winter, you might opt for a rustic bistro menu, or a Sunday roast with all the trimmings. For a bit of fun, how about a retro or French-themed dinner party? Or for a special celebration, a seafood banquet is hard to beat. Feel free to adapt these menus and play around with different combinations. For the best results, I recommend you use produce which is in season. Not only is it easier to get, but it also tastes better, is better-quality and better-priced too.

My life is pretty frantic these days, with my various work commitments; I'm sure yours is the same. That makes time spent with family and friends all the more precious, and every dinner party a special occasion. I hope that you enjoy this book as much as I have enjoyed putting it together.

MATT

DRINKS
AND
APPETISERS

OYSTERS WITH MIGNONETTE DRESSING

SERVES 12 (2 PER PERSON)

Pacific oysters and Sydney rock oysters are the main types available in Australia. I prefer Sydney rock oysters, which are smaller, have a milder taste and are at their best from September to March. During the cooler months you might prefer to use Pacific oysters, which peak from April to September.

---

3 golden shallots, very finely chopped
100 ml aged red wine vinegar
1 teaspoon freshly ground black pepper
24 oysters, freshly shucked
rock salt, to serve
lemon wedges, to serve (optional)

---

1 To make the dressing, combine the shallots, red wine vinegar and black pepper in a bowl and stir to combine. The dressing can be made in advance and stored in the fridge for up to 2 days.

2 To serve, place the freshly shucked oysters on a bed of rock salt. Spoon the dressing over the oysters, and serve with lemon wedges if you like.

OYSTERS WITH PEACH AND GINGER VINEGAR

SERVES 12 (2 PER PERSON)

This is a fresh and slightly different way to serve oysters. Ginger vinegar is available from specialty delis, but if you can't find it, make your own by mixing ½ cup (125 ml) pickled ginger juice with ½ cup (125 ml) rice wine vinegar and 1 teaspoon sugar.

---

1 yellow peach, cut in half, stone removed,
    flesh cut into 5 mm pieces
¼ long cucumber, peeled, seeded and
    flesh cut into 5 mm pieces
2 teaspoons chopped coriander leaves,
    plus extra leaves to garnish
24 oysters, freshly shucked
rock salt, to serve
1 cup (250 ml) ginger vinegar

---

1 Combine the peach and cucumber in a bowl, then gently stir through the coriander.

2 To serve, place the freshly shucked oysters on a bed of rock salt. Spoon an equal amount of the peach mixture onto each oyster, then drizzle over a little ginger vinegar and garnish with extra coriander.

WHITE PEACH BELLINI

SERVES 4

The Bellini, named after the fifteenth-century Venetian painter Giovanni Bellini, was invented by the owner of the famous Harry's Bar in Venice. For best results, make sure the glasses, peach nectar and prosecco are all as cold as possible. You can store any leftover peach puree in an airtight container in the fridge for up to three days.

---

1 white peach, cut in half, stone removed
50 ml peach nectar
440 ml prosecco, chilled

---

1 Peel away the skin of the peach using a small, sharp knife and place the flesh in a blender with the peach nectar. Blend until smooth.

2 Pour approximately 1 tablespoon of the puree into each of four champagne flutes, then top up with the prosecco. Gently stir then serve.

MALDIVIAN MANGO

SERVES 4

This is a great party-starter – fresh and delicious, with a little kick. Vanilla-infused sugar is handy to have in your pantry – you can add a teaspoon to your coffee or hot chocolate, sprinkle it over fresh strawberries, or use it instead of plain caster sugar when making cakes and biscuits.

---

1 mango, peeled, stone removed,
    flesh roughly chopped
¾ cup (180 ml) ginger wine
¾ cup (180 ml) dark rum
juice of 3 lemons
1 cup ice cubes
6 sprigs mint

VANILLA-INFUSED SUGAR
1 vanilla bean, split and beans scraped
300 g caster sugar

---

1 To make the vanilla-infused sugar, mix the ingredients together and store in an airtight container.

2 Puree the mango flesh in a blender until smooth. Add the ginger wine, rum, 2 tablespoons vanilla-infused sugar, lemon juice and the ice and blend until smooth.

3 Pour into four chilled martini glasses, garnish with a sprig of mint then serve.

TOMATO AND FETA SALAD WITH BASIL AND GREEN OLIVES

SERVES 6

You can use any type of tomato for this salad – I like to use a combination of heirloom, truss, cherry and vine-ripened. Take them out of the fridge an hour before you use them, so that they are at room temperature when you serve them. When I can get it I use barrel-aged feta. Made from a blend of sheep's and goat's milk and aged in birch barrels, it's available at specialty grocers.

¼ red onion, peeled and thinly sliced
salt and pepper
1 tablespoon red wine vinegar
1 kg tomatoes
¼ sourdough baguette
3 tablespoons olive oil
½ cup (80 g) green olives, pitted and roughly chopped
100 g feta, crumbled
6 basil leaves

---

1 Preheat the oven grill to its highest temperature.

2 Rinse the red onion under cold running water for approximately 20 seconds to remove the raw taste. Drain well, then pat dry with paper towel and place in a bowl. Season with salt and pepper, then pour in the red wine vinegar and toss to coat. Set aside.

3 Remove the cores from the tomatoes using a small paring knife and cut the flesh into wedges.

4 Thinly slice the baguette and place in a bowl with a tablespoon of olive oil. Season with salt and pepper and toss to coat. Place the bread on a baking tray under the hot grill for about 1 minute until golden brown. Turn over and repeat on the other side. Remove from the grill and allow to cool.

5 To serve, arrange the tomato on a large serving platter and top with the sourdough croutons, red onion, olives and crumbled feta. Tear the basil leaves and scatter over the salad. Drizzle with the remaining olive oil, season with salt and pepper and serve.

PEACHES WRAPPED IN SERRANO HAM

SERVES 4

Serrano is a Spanish cured ham available from specialty delis. It is worth seeking out for the flavour it gives this simple dish. If you can't find any, prosciutto is a good substitute.

---

2 white peaches
8 thin slices Serrano ham

---

1 Cut the peaches in half and remove the stone, then cut each peach into quarters.

2 Wrap a piece of ham around each peach quarter, then serve as an accompaniment to a white peach Bellini (see page 8).

TARTARE OF KINGFISH WITH TOMATO JELLY

SERVES 8–10

This is a sensational appetiser. You need to start making the tomato jelly the day before. Ideally, buy the kingfish on the day you plan to serve it.

---

400 g kingfish fillet, skin and
    bloodline removed, flesh cut
    into 5 mm dice
2 tablespoons extra virgin olive oil
salt and pepper
4 cherry tomatoes, cut into quarters
basil, to garnish

TOMATO JELLY
450 g roma tomatoes, chopped
1 small stalk celery (from the inner
    heart of the bunch), chopped
¼ small red onion, chopped
½ clove garlic
10 basil leaves
1 teaspoon Worcestershire sauce

1 teaspoon good quality
    red wine vinegar
½ teaspoon Tabasco sauce
2½ leaves gold-strength gelatine

---

1 To make the tomato jelly, place all the ingredients except the gelatine in a food processor and process the mixture to a very smooth puree.

2 Place a large colander or sieve lined with muslin over a large bowl. Pour the puree into the colander or sieve and leave it to stand overnight, or until 1 cup (250 ml) of clear liquid has dripped into the bowl – do not press down on the solids or the mixture will turn cloudy.

3 Place the cup of clear liquid into a saucepan and bring almost to a simmer.

4 Soften the gelatine in cold water for a minute or so, then remove and squeeze with your fingers to remove excess water.

5 Remove the saucepan from the heat and stir in the gelatine until dissolved. Transfer the mixture to a bowl and refrigerate for 3 hours or until set to a soft, wobbly consistency.

6 In a bowl, combine the fish with the olive oil, salt and pepper and stir gently.

7 Divide the fish among 8–10 shot glasses, then spoon some jelly on top. Scatter over the tomato quarters and basil and serve immediately.

DUCK RILLETTES WITH SAFFRON PICKLED ONIONS

SERVES 6

This recipe makes a big batch of pickled onions, which will keep for some time in the fridge and are great to have on hand to serve with cold meats or to spice up a cheese sandwich. If you want to keep them for longer, store them in a sterilised preserving jar; they will last for months. (To sterilise jars for preserving, I submerge them in boiling water for 2 minutes, then leave them to drip-dry.) The leftover cooking liquid (rendered fat) from the rillettes can be strained and placed in an airtight container and will last in the fridge for a few months. This can be used to turn ordinary roast potatoes into something really special; just add a couple of spoonfuls of fat to the potatoes in the roasting tray.

1 kg (about 4) duck marylands
    (leg and thigh portions)
2 tablespoons salt
2 sprigs thyme
1 fresh bay leaf
1 sprig rosemary
100 g pork back fat, chopped
100 g duck fat
2 tablespoons white wine
1 teaspoon black peppercorns
3 cloves garlic, bruised
½ carrot, in one piece

olive oil, to cover, optional
1 small sourdough baguette,
    thinly sliced
2 tablespoons olive oil
sea salt, to taste

SAFFRON PICKLED ONIONS
2 cups (500 ml) rice wine vinegar
200 g caster sugar
½ teaspoon cloves
2 teaspoons salt
1 teaspoon yellow mustard seeds

1 teaspoon black peppercorns
1 × 3 cm piece ginger, sliced
1 small red chilli
1 clove garlic
½ teaspoon coriander seeds
½ teaspoon cumin seeds
2 sprigs curry leaves
large pinch of saffron threads
½ teaspoon fennel seeds
1 kg pickling onions, peeled,
    leaving tips and roots intact
    so they retain their shape

1 To make the saffron pickled onions, combine all the ingredients except the onions in a large heavy-based saucepan or stockpot. Bring to a simmer over low heat and then add the onions. Bring the mixture back to a simmer and cook over low heat for 40 minutes until just tender.

2 Meanwhile, preheat the oven to 120°C. Sprinkle the duck marylands with the 2 tablespoons salt and chill in the fridge for 1 hour.

3 Tie the herbs together using kitchen string, then throw them into a large, heavy-based casserole along with the chopped pork fat, duck fat, white wine, peppercorns, garlic, carrot and 200 ml water. The ingredients should be completely covered by the liquid; if not, top up with olive oil to cover. Place the lid on and transfer the casserole to the oven to cook for 1 hour, or until the fat has mostly rendered (melted).

4 Rinse the salt from the duck marylands under cold running water and add them to the casserole. Cover, return to the oven and cook for 4 hours or until the marylands are very tender.

5 Remove the casserole from the oven, increasing the oven temperature to 180°C. When cool enough to handle, transfer the duck marylands to a chopping board, discarding the herbs and reserving the cooking liquid.

6 Separate the duck meat from the bones, shredding it with your fingers, and transfer to a bowl, discarding the bones and skin. Remove the carrot and garlic from the cooking liquid, grate or very finely chop them, and add to the bowl with the duck meat.

7 Strain half the reserved cooking liquid over the duck meat and season to taste. Refrigerate the remaining cooking liquid for another use. Half-fill a larger bowl with ice, then nestle the bowl containing the duck meat in the bowl of ice, stirring every 5 minutes or so with a spatula until cool and the fat has emulsified.

8 Place the baguette slices on an oven tray, drizzle with the olive oil and sprinkle with sea salt. Bake for 5–6 minutes or until golden and crisp.

9 Serve the rillettes spooned onto toast, with some pickled onions alongside.

PORK AND PISTACHIO TERRINE WITH PEACH CHUTNEY

SERVES 10

Cooking terrines evenly all the way through can be tricky, so my tip is to place a tea towel under the mould in the baking dish to help disperse the heat consistently. I also like to use freezer film to line the mould, as it is strong enough to hold the terrine together as you lift it. Stored in a sterilised preserving jar (see page 13), the peach chutney will keep in the fridge for months. Serve it with cold meats, roast pork or even just a chunk of cheese and a crusty bread roll.

---

30 g butter
1 onion, finely diced
2 cloves garlic, finely chopped
750 g pork shoulder, coarsely minced
250 g chicken livers, trimmed and
    coarsely minced
500 g pork fat, coarsely minced
½ bunch sage, finely chopped
1 teaspoon ground allspice
⅓ cup (50 g) pistachios, roughly chopped
3 teaspoons salt
1½ teaspoons freshly ground black pepper

canola oil, for spraying
400 g thinly sliced speck, rind removed
fresh peach slices, olive oil, baby
    watercress (optional) and sliced
    crusty bread, to serve

PEACH CHUTNEY
1 very ripe roma tomato
5–6 yellow peaches
1 small granny smith apple,
    peeled, cored and grated
½ teaspoon salt

½ small onion, finely chopped
finely grated zest and juice of 1 lime
150 g caster sugar
½ teaspoon ground cinnamon
½ teaspoon ground nutmeg
½ teaspoon ground white pepper
1 clove garlic, finely chopped
boiling water, to fill roasting tin
1 × 2 cm piece ginger, peeled
    and finely chopped
150 ml white wine vinegar
½ cup (40 g) flaked almonds

---

1 To make the chutney, use a small, sharp knife to cut a cross in the base of the tomato. Bring plenty of water to the boil in a saucepan, add the tomato and blanch for about 30 seconds, then transfer to a bowl of iced water. Drain well, then peel the tomato and cut into quarters. Remove the seeds and chop the flesh. Meanwhile, add the peaches to the boiling water for 1 minute then remove using a slotted spoon. Plunge into the bowl of iced water then drain well. Peel off the skin then cut the peaches in half, remove the stone and cut the flesh into small pieces. Set aside.

2 Combine all the chutney ingredients except the peaches in a large heavy-based saucepan and bring to a simmer over low heat, stirring occasionally. Cook for 30 minutes or until the mixture has reduced to a jam-like consistency, then add the peaches. Cook over low–medium heat, stirring often, for 40 minutes or until very thick. Transfer to sterilised jars (see page 13) then leave to cool slightly before sealing.

3 To make the terrine, preheat the oven to 160°C. Melt the butter in a saucepan over medium heat then add the onion and garlic and cook, stirring often, for 5–6 minutes or until softened. Remove to a bowl and leave to cool. Add the minced meats, sage, allspice, pistachios and salt and pepper to the bowl and combine well. Spray a 2 litre capacity terrine mould with canola oil. Cut out a piece of freezer film large enough to line the base and sides of the mould and lay it flat on a benchtop. Layer the speck on the film, completely covering the surface (you should have some left over), then place another sheet of freezer film on top. Lift the whole lot and place into the terrine, pressing down on the base and sides and pushing the lining into the corners, then carefully peel off the top layer of film.

4 Pack the meat mixture into the mould, taking care not to disturb the speck lining, and smooth the top. Bring any overhanging pieces of speck up and over the mixture to enclose, then use the remaining speck to completely cover the surface of the terrine. Cover the terrine tightly in foil then place the lid on top. Place a folded clean tea towel in the base of a roasting tin large enough to fit the mould. Place the mould on top of the tea towel and pour in enough boiling water to come halfway up the sides of the mould. Bake for 50 minutes or until the juices run clear when the terrine is pierced in the middle with a skewer, then remove from the oven and leave to rest for 10–15 minutes.

5 Transfer the mould to a large dish, place a chopping board on top then weight evenly with cans of food or similar. Cool to room temperature then refrigerate overnight.

6 Remove the weights and foil, take hold of the freezer film and carefully lift the terrine out of the mould. Peel off the freezer film and thickly slice the terrine. Serve with peach slices drizzled with olive oil and garnished with watercress. Accompany with the peach chutney and some crusty bread.

BEETROOT-CURED OCEAN TROUT WITH PICKLED BEETS

SERVES 6

This is a show-stopping appetiser (pictured overleaf) that works equally well in summer and winter. You can prepare the ocean trout well in advance and store it in the fridge until you are ready to use it. This recipe makes a large amount of pickling liquid (about 1.7 litres), but you can use the leftovers to pickle all sorts of vegetables, including cauliflower, carrots and cucumber. Stored in sterilised preserving jars (see page 13), these keep for weeks and can be used to throw together a mezze plate at a moment's notice. For the pickled beets, you can use one type of beet or a variety. I like using target beets because they look great when cut. Make sure you wash the beets really well before you use them – I soak them in cold water for 10–15 minutes to get rid of any dirt or grit.

1 side ocean trout (approximately
   1.2 kg), scaled and pin-boned
1 bunch golden beets,
   well washed and trimmed
1 bunch target beets,
   well washed and trimmed
1 bunch baby red beets,
   well washed and trimmed
1¼ tablespoons olive oil
¼ teaspoon xanthan gum
   (available from health food
   shops and some delicatessens)
1 small handful frisee (curly endive)
1 small handful beetroot leaves
extra virgin olive oil, for drizzling
sea salt, to serve

CURING MIX
1 large beetroot, peeled and grated
grated zest and juice of 1 orange
grated zest and juice of 1 lemon
½ bunch flat-leaf parsley, leaves picked
½ bunch basil, leaves picked
½ bunch coriander, leaves picked
1 bunch dill
150 g salt flakes
100 g sugar
2 tablespoons black peppercorns

PICKLING LIQUID
600 ml rice wine vinegar
125 g caster sugar
3 cloves
2 tablespoons table salt
1 tablespoon yellow mustard seeds
10 black peppercorns
1 × 2 cm piece ginger, chopped
1 large red chilli, halved lengthways
1 Serrano chilli, halved lengthways
1 clove garlic, sliced

1 To make the curing mix, place all the ingredients in a small food processor and blitz until well combined.

2 Place the ocean trout, skin-side down, on a piece of plastic film large enough to enclose the fish. Spread the curing mix all over the flesh-side of the fish, then wrap tightly in the plastic film, and wrap in a few more layers of plastic film to ensure it is tightly sealed. Place on a tray in the fridge to cure for 36 hours.

3 To make the pickling liquid, place all the ingredients in a large saucepan along with 1 litre water and bring to the boil. Reduce the heat to low and simmer for 30 minutes to allow the flavours to infuse, then set aside to cool.

4 Place the golden and target beets in a saucepan and the baby beets in a separate saucepan (so they don't stain each other). Pour enough pickling liquid into each saucepan to cover the beets, transfer to the stove and bring to the boil over high heat. Reduce the heat to medium and simmer for about 5–7 minutes or until the beets are soft but still have some firmness – you don't want them to be overcooked. Remove from the heat and allow the beets to cool in the liquid, then peel off the skins.

5 Place the peeled beets in three 1 litre sterilised jars and pour over enough pickling liquid to cover, then seal and store in the fridge until ready to use. Reserve any unused pickling liquid in the fridge for another use.

6 Unwrap the fish and rinse under cold water until completely clean. Pat dry with paper towel, then rub the flesh with olive oil. Wrap in a fresh layer of plastic film and refrigerate until ready to use.

7 Transfer about 100 ml of pickling liquid from the beets into a bowl and sprinkle in the xanthan gum. Whisk to combine, then set aside for 10–15 minutes to allow the mixture to thicken. Whisk again until you have a smooth sauce.

8 To serve, slice the fish thinly, trim off the skin and arrange on a plate with the salad leaves and some sliced or whole pickled beets. Dress with a few drops of sauce and some extra virgin olive oil and finish with a scattering of sea salt.

COD BRANDADE WITH MUSSELS

SERVES 6

Brandade was invented in France in the early nineteenth century. It is quite rich, so is best served before a lighter main course. You can use snapper in place of the cod if you like. When cooking mussels, my tip is not to throw out any stubborn ones that do not open. Despite what many people think, they are not off – often they just need a little extra cooking time. (Of course, discard them if they don't smell quite right.)

12 × 5 mm thick slices
   sourdough bread
olive oil, for brushing
225 ml extra virgin olive oil
½ bulb garlic
5 sprigs flat-leaf parsley
3 sprigs thyme

2½ tablespoons white wine
1 kg black mussels, scrubbed
   and debearded
2 golden shallots, finely sliced
2½ tablespoons red wine vinegar
1½ tablespoons baby capers, rinsed
1 tablespoon chopped flat-leaf parsley

BRANDADE
500 g piece cod fillet,
   pin-boned and skin removed
80 g table salt
1 large desiree potato, peeled
   and quartered
4–5 cloves garlic
2 sprigs thyme
200 ml cream
800 ml milk, plus more if needed
2 teaspoons truffle oil
salt and pepper

1 For the brandade, place the fish in a non-reactive dish, skin-side down, and sprinkle over the salt. Refrigerate for 30 minutes, then rinse well and pat dry with paper towel.

2 Meanwhile, cook the potato in boiling salted water until tender. Drain well, then push through a potato ricer or a fine-meshed sieve into a large bowl and set aside.

3 Place the fish in a large saucepan and add the garlic, thyme, cream and enough milk to cover. Bring to a simmer then turn off the heat and leave the fish to stand in the milk for 10 minutes or until cooked through. Remove the fish with a slotted spoon and set aside to cool slightly. Strain the cooking liquid into a measuring cup or jug, discarding the solids.

4 When the fish is cool enough to handle, remove the flesh and flake it finely, removing any remaining bones. Add the fish to the potato and mix well, then stir in the truffle oil and about ½ cup (125 ml) of the cooking liquid until you get a soft but firm consistency. Season to taste, then transfer to a serving bowl and leave to stand at room temperature while you toast the bread and cook the mussels.

5 Preheat the oven to 200°C. Brush some oil over the sourdough slices then toast them on a baking tray in the oven for 3–5 minutes until golden.

6 Meanwhile, place 100 ml of the extra virgin olive oil, the garlic, parsley and thyme sprigs and white wine in a large saucepan over high heat. Add the mussels and cover with a tight-fitting lid, then cook, shaking the pan often, for 3–4 minutes or until the mussels open. Drain the mussels well, discarding the cooking liquid. Allow the mussels to cool slightly, then remove the mussel meat from the shells and set aside.

7 Heat the remaining 125 ml extra virgin olive oil in a saucepan over medium heat, add the shallot and cook, stirring, for 2 minutes or until the shallot is just beginning to soften. Add the mussels, vinegar, capers and chopped parsley and stir to make a warm dressing, then remove from the heat.

8 Spoon the mussels and dressing over the brandade and serve with the sourdough toast on the side.

LAMB AND HARISSA SAUSAGE ROLLS

MAKES 16

Inspired by the legendary Bourke Street Bakery in Sydney, this is an adults' version of the kids' all-time party favourite – sausage rolls. Harissa is a hot chilli paste that's very popular in North African cooking, and here it gives the lamb a delicious spicy flavour. It is very handy to keep in the pantry as it can liven up many dishes. These sausage rolls are wonderful served with a yoghurt-based dipping sauce such as tzatziki.

---

20 g butter
1 brown onion, finely chopped
2 teaspoons ground coriander
2 teaspoons ground cumin
250 g lamb shoulder, minced (ask your butcher to do this for you)

150 g pork and fennel sausage meat
1 tablespoon harissa
50 g slivered almonds
1 preserved lemon, rind only, rinsed and finely chopped
20 mint leaves, finely chopped

2 sheets puff pastry (thawed if frozen)
1 egg, lightly whisked with 2 teaspoons water
2 teaspoons sea salt flakes
2 teaspoons cumin seeds

---

1 Melt the butter in a saucepan over low heat, then add the onion and cook, stirring occasionally, for 7–8 minutes or until softened. Add the ground spices and cook, stirring, for 2 minutes or until fragrant. Remove the pan from the heat.

2 In a large mixing bowl, combine the onion mixture with the minced lamb, sausage meat, harissa, almonds, lemon and mint with your hands. Divide the mixture into four even-sized portions.

3 Preheat the oven to 180°C and line a baking tray with non-stick baking paper.

4 Cut each sheet of pastry in half widthways. Working with one piece of pastry and one portion of meat mixture at a time, place the meat in a strip down the middle of the pastry. Brush the edges of the pastry lightly with the egg mixture, then carefully roll the pastry around the meat to form a log, gently pressing on the join to seal and trimming away any excess pastry as necessary. Repeat with the remaining pastry and meat, then place the logs on the tray, seam-side down, and brush all over with the egg mixture. Sprinkle with salt and cumin seeds and bake for 30 minutes.

5 Remove the sausage rolls from the oven and cool on the tray for 2–3 minutes, then transfer to a chopping board. Using a large sharp knife, cut each roll into four and serve.

SOUPS

LOBSTER BISQUE WITH ORANGE AND CARDAMOM

SERVES 8

This is a real special-occasion dish but it is not at all difficult to make. You can get lobster shells from fish markets, or, if you ever treat yourself to lobster, just save the shells in the freezer to use later to make stock. It is definitely worth using homemade stock if you can.

1.5 kg lobster shells
¼ cup (60 ml) vegetable oil
1 carrot, chopped
2 stalks celery, chopped
1 small bulb fennel, chopped
1 onion, chopped
6 cloves garlic, halved
1 small desiree potato, chopped
1 roma tomato, chopped and seeded

2½ tablespoons tomato paste
2½ tablespoons brandy
2½ tablespoons dry vermouth
   (I like to use Noilly Prat)
2.5 litres chicken stock
   (see page 222)
1 orange, rind and white pith
   removed, rind cut into pieces
   about 1½ cm wide

2½ teaspoons cardamom pods, bruised
1 star anise
few sprigs tarragon, leaves picked,
   stalks reserved
2 cups (500 ml) pouring cream
lemon juice, to taste
freshly ground black pepper
crusty bread, to serve

---

1 Using a meat mallet or the end of a rolling pin, smash the lobster shells to break them up into small pieces.

2 Heat half the vegetable oil over medium heat in a stockpot or a very large heavy-based saucepan. Add the smashed lobster shells and cook for 10 minutes or until they have turned orange.

3 Meanwhile, heat the remaining oil in a large frying pan over medium–high heat. Add the carrot, celery, fennel, onion, garlic and potato and cook, stirring occasionally, for 15 minutes or until the vegetables are golden. Add the chopped tomato and tomato paste and cook, stirring, for 2 minutes. Transfer this mixture to the stockpot with the lobster and stir.

4 Return the frying pan to the heat, add the brandy and dry vermouth and bring to the boil over high heat, stirring and scraping the base of the pan to dislodge any stuck-on bits (add a little of the chicken stock to moisten the pan further if necessary). Pour this mixture into the stockpot,

along with the rest of the chicken stock and the orange rind, cardamom, star anise and tarragon stalks. Bring the mixture to a simmer, skimming off any scum that rises to the surface, then reduce the heat to low and cook for 45 minutes, skimming often.

5 Working in batches, strain the soup through a fine-meshed sieve placed over a saucepan, pressing down on the mixture as firmly as you can with a ladle to extract as much of the liquid as possible. Discard the solids, then transfer the strained soup to the stove, bring to a simmer and cook over low–medium heat for 45 minutes or until reduced by a third.

6 Add the cream and simmer for 10 minutes then remove the pan from the heat. Stir in lemon juice to taste.

7 Using a hand-held blender, puree the soup until silky smooth, then divide among warmed soup bowls. Sprinkle over the tarragon leaves and finish with a twist of black pepper, then serve with crusty bread.

SMOKED HAM BROTH WITH CABBAGE AND QUAIL EGGS

SERVES 6

The combination of ham and cabbage gives this broth a very rich flavour, and the boiled quail eggs add a touch of delicacy. The quail eggs will be easier to peel if you dunk them in cold water immediately after boiling.

1½ tablespoons vegetable oil
1 onion, chopped
1 stalk celery, halved
½ leek, halved
1 carrot, halved
3 cloves garlic, halved
1 fresh bay leaf

1 sprig thyme
1 large ham hock (about 1 kg)
1 kg ham bones
3 litres chicken stock (see page 222)
¼ small Savoy cabbage, tough outer
   leaves discarded, tender inner leaves
   cut into strips

12 quail eggs
1 tablespoon extra virgin olive oil
1 tablespoon finely chopped chives

---

1 Heat the vegetable oil in a large stockpot, add the onion and cook over medium heat, stirring occasionally, for 8 minutes or until golden. Add the celery, leek, carrot, garlic, bay leaf, thyme, ham hock, bones and chicken stock and bring to a simmer, skimming off any scum that forms on the surface. Reduce the heat to low and simmer for 3 hours, skimming the surface occasionally.

2 Remove the pot from the heat and transfer the ham hock to a chopping board. Strain the cooking liquid through a fine-meshed sieve into a saucepan, discarding the solids, and keep warm over low heat.

3 Cook the cabbage in a large saucepan of boiling salted water for 2–3 minutes or until softened, then drain well and set aside.

4 Bring another saucepan of water to the boil, add the quail eggs and boil for 1 minute 40 seconds. Remove with a slotted spoon and, when the eggs are cool enough to handle, peel off the shells. Cut them in half or leave them whole, whichever you prefer.

5 Meanwhile, when the ham hock is cool enough to handle, remove the meat from the bones, discarding any skin or gristle, and finely shred the meat with your fingers.

6 Divide the cabbage, shredded ham and quail eggs among six bowls, then ladle over the broth. To finish, drizzle with olive oil, sprinkle with chives and serve immediately.

SWEETCORN AND LEMONGRASS SOUP

SERVES 4–6

This soup has a delicious, citrussy flavour and a silky-smooth texture that is achieved by straining it through a sieve just before serving. I like to use Kara coconut cream as it gives a super-creamy result.

---

4 sweetcorn, husks and silks removed
1.25 litres chicken stock (see page 222)
2½ tablespoons vegetable oil
65 g butter
2 onions, diced
1 large potato, diced
salt
baby coriander sprigs or regular
    coriander, to garnish

COCONUT SAUCE
1 × 3 cm piece galangal, chopped
1 × 3 cm piece ginger, chopped
1 golden shallot, sliced
6 coriander roots, chopped
1 bird's eye chilli, seeded and chopped
½ stick lemongrass,
    white part only, sliced
2 tablespoons vegetable oil

300 ml coconut cream
1 tablespoon lime juice
3 teaspoons fish sauce,
    or to taste
freshly ground black pepper

---

1 Place a corn cob upright on a chopping board and, with a sharp knife, carefully cut downwards along the cob to remove the kernels. Repeat with the remaining cobs, transfer the kernels to a bowl and set aside.

2 Place the cobs and the chicken stock in a large saucepan and bring to the boil over high heat. Reduce the heat to low and simmer for 20 minutes, then strain the stock into a jug, discarding the cobs.

3 Meanwhile, heat the oil and butter in a large heavy-based saucepan over medium heat. Once the butter has melted, add the onion, potato and a pinch of salt and cook, stirring occasionally, for 10 minutes or until the vegetables have softened but not coloured. Add the corn kernels and the strained stock, bring to a simmer then cook over low–medium heat for 20–30 minutes or until the vegetables are very tender.

4 Transfer the soup to a blender or food processor and puree until smooth, then push the soup through a fine-meshed sieve into a clean saucepan to remove any small lumps. Season to taste, cover and place on the stove over low heat just to keep warm.

5 Meanwhile, to make the coconut sauce, combine the galangal, ginger, shallot, coriander root, chilli, lemongrass and half the vegetable oil in a food processor or blender and process to a coarse paste.

6 Heat the remaining vegetable oil in a small saucepan over medium heat, add the paste and cook, stirring, for 2 minutes or until fragrant. Add the coconut cream and bring to a simmer, then cook, stirring, for 2 minutes or until thickened. Remove the pan from the heat, stir through the lime juice and fish sauce, then season with pepper and a little more fish sauce to taste, if necessary. Strain the mixture through a sieve, discarding the solids (add a tablespoon or two of water if the sauce seems too thick).

7 Ladle the soup into individual warmed bowls. Lightly whisk the coconut sauce then spoon some into each bowl. Scatter over a few sprigs of coriander before serving.

CASUAL SUNDAY ROAST

SERVES 6–8

What's not to love about a good, old-fashioned Sunday roast with a group of close friends or family? The ras el hanout adds a lovely spicy flavour to the soup, and the pork loin is great roasted – and a bit different from the usual lamb or chicken. Finish it all off with some indulgent steamed puddings, best served piping hot.

Split Pea Soup with Ras el Hanout	**36**
Roast Pork Loin with Jerusalem Artichoke Puree and Caramelised Pears	**131**
Steamed Mandarin and Treacle Puddings	**198**

A SUMMER BARBECUE

SERVES 6

I love getting a group of friends together on a beautiful summer's evening for a long, lazy night by the barbecue. I serve a selection of light dishes before progressing to that all-time family favourite – a hamburger with all the trimmings. Give your friends a little break, then delight them with the grilled pineapple, which packs quite a punch with its chilli syrup.

SPLIT PEA SOUP WITH RAS EL HANOUT

SERVES 6

Ras el hanout is a combination of spices often used in North African cooking. It means literally 'top of the shop', that is, the best spices available. This makes more than you'll need for this recipe – store the remainder in an airtight container and you'll have it on hand to add to braises, rice or couscous dishes or to rub into meats prior to cooking. Start this recipe the day before, as the split peas need to soak overnight.

---

375 g yellow split peas
50 g butter
1 onion, chopped
1 carrot, chopped
1 leek, trimmed, well washed
   and chopped
2 cloves garlic, chopped

1 long red chilli, chopped
3 litres vegetable stock (see page 222)
salt and pepper
100 g Greek-style yoghurt
baby coriander sprigs or regular
   coriander, to garnish

RAS EL HANOUT
1 tablespoon ground cumin
1 tablespoon ground ginger
1 tablespoon table salt
3 teaspoons freshly ground
   black pepper
2 teaspoons ground cinnamon
2 teaspoons ground coriander
2 teaspoons cayenne pepper
1 teaspoon ground cloves
2 teaspoons ground fennel seeds

---

1 Soak the split peas in cold water overnight, then drain well.

2 To make the ras el hanout, mix all the ingredients together and store in an airtight container.

3 Melt the butter in a large saucepan over medium heat, add the onion, carrot, leek, garlic and chilli and cook, stirring often, for 10 minutes or until the vegetables have softened. Add 1½ tablespoons ras el hanout and cook, stirring, for 1–2 minutes or until fragrant, then add the split peas and the vegetable stock. Bring to the boil, skimming off any scum that forms on the surface, then reduce the heat to low and cook for about 1 hour or until the peas are very tender.

4 Working in batches, transfer the soup to a blender or food processor and blend until very smooth, then strain through a fine-meshed sieve, discarding any solids.

5 Season to taste with salt and pepper then divide among warmed bowls. Add a spoonful of yoghurt and scatter over the coriander, then serve immediately.

BOUILLABAISSE

SERVES 8

The origins of this creamy fish soup are much debated and there are now many different versions, but most have in common the use of Provencal spices and herbs like saffron and thyme, and are usually served with a thick garlicky sauce called a rouille. As well as the more traditional white wine, I like to use Pernod to add a hint of aniseed to the taste.

100 ml olive oil
1 carrot, chopped
1 bulb fennel, trimmed and chopped
1 brown onion, chopped
1 stalk celery, chopped
7 cloves garlic, 6 crushed, 1 cut in half
2 star anise
large pinch of saffron threads
2 sprigs thyme
1 bay leaf
salt and pepper
6 vine-ripened tomatoes, cut in half,
    seeds removed
1 cup (280 g) tomato paste

100 ml Pernod
1 cup (250 ml) white wine
2 floury potatoes (such as
    desiree), sliced
500 g flathead fillets, pin-boned and
    skin removed, cut into 5 cm pieces
2 red mullet fillets (or rock cod),
    scales removed, cut into 8 pieces
1.5 kg white fish bones (such as cod
    or snapper), roughly chopped
2 sprigs basil, leaves picked
juice of 1 lemon
8 slices baguette
grated gruyere, to serve

ROUILLE
1 floury potato (such as desiree)
large pinch of saffron threads
1 tablespoon white wine vinegar
1 egg yolk
2 teaspoons hot English mustard
1 clove garlic, crushed
salt and pepper
100 ml extra virgin olive oil
100 ml grapeseed oil
juice of 1 lemon

1 Heat the olive oil in a large, heavy-based saucepan over medium heat for 2 minutes then add the carrot, fennel, onion, celery, crushed garlic, star anise, saffron, thyme and bay leaf. Season with salt and pepper then cook for 5 minutes. Add the tomato and tomato paste then continue to cook, stirring, for a further 5 minutes. Pour in the Pernod and white wine, then bring the mixture to a simmer and cook for 10 minutes or until nearly all the liquid has evaporated. Add the potato, chopped fish and fish bones then pour over enough water to cover. Bring the liquid to the boil, skimming away any oil and scum that floats to the surface, then lower the heat to a gentle simmer. Cook for 2½ hours, skimming the surface often.

2 Once cooked, ladle the soup into a blender and lightly puree to break down the fish bones a little. Strain the soup through a fine-meshed sieve into a clean saucepan, pressing down firmly to extract as much liquid as possible, then discard the solids. Return the soup to the stove and bring to the boil, skimming away any scum that forms on the surface. Leave the soup to boil rapidly for 10 minutes. Add the basil leaves, lemon juice and a little more seasoning if required, then remove from the heat and set aside to infuse for 2 minutes before straining again through a fine-meshed sieve.

3 For the rouille, cook the potato in boiling salted water until tender. Drain, then push the potato through a sieve or potato ricer. Set aside until required.

4 Combine the saffron and white wine vinegar in a small saucepan then bring to the boil. Remove from the heat and allow to cool.

5 In a bowl, whisk the egg yolk, mustard, garlic and seasoning together. Add the oils in a slow trickle, whisking continuously until all the oil has been incorporated and the mixture is thick (take care not to add the oils too quickly or the sauce will separate). Stir in the saffron-infused vinegar, the potato and the juice of half a lemon and whisk until smooth. Season to taste with salt and pepper and a little more lemon juice if necessary.

6 Just before you are ready to serve, toast the baguette slices and rub with the cut side of the garlic halves.

7 Gently reheat the bouillabaisse and serve with the baguette slices, grated gruyere and rouille on the side.

MUSHROOM CONSOMME WITH TARRAGON

SERVES 6–8

This is an elegant, flavoursome soup. To get the texture just right, and to remove fat and any other impurities, you need to clarify the stock. While this takes a little more time, the result – a clear, pure consomme – is well worth the effort.

---

20 g dried porcini mushrooms
boiling water, for soaking
¼ cup (60 ml) vegetable oil
1.2 kg chicken wings, coarsely chopped
  (ask your butcher to do this for you)
250 g large flat mushrooms, sliced
1 onion, chopped
1 bulb garlic, cloves separated, peeled
  and bruised with the flat part
  of a large knife

2 stalks celery, chopped
2.25 litres chicken stock (see page 222)
150 ml Madeira
2 sprigs thyme
125 g chicken breast fillet, chopped
3 egg whites
100 g enoki mushrooms, trimmed
16 shiitake mushrooms, finely sliced
2 king brown mushrooms, bases sliced
  and tops quartered

2 teaspoons black truffle oil
1 tablespoon tarragon leaves
shaved black truffle, to serve, optional

---

1 Place the porcini mushrooms in a small bowl, cover with boiling water and leave to stand for 20 minutes or until softened. Drain well, reserving the soaking liquid. Strain the liquid through a muslin-lined sieve.

2 Heat 1½ tablespoons of the oil in a large, heavy-based frying pan over medium heat. Working in batches if necessary, add the chicken wings and cook, turning often, for 10 minutes or until browned all over.

3 Meanwhile, heat the remaining oil in a large saucepan over medium heat, add the sliced mushroom, onion, garlic and celery and cook, stirring often, for 10 minutes or until golden. Add the chicken stock, Madeira, thyme, the drained porcini, the strained soaking liquid and the browned chicken wings. Bring the mixture to a simmer, skimming off any scum that rises to the surface, then reduce the heat to low and cook for 1 hour, skimming occasionally. Once cooked, strain through a muslin-lined sieve, discarding the solids, and set aside to cool to room temperature.

4 Place the chopped chicken breast and the egg whites into a food processor and blend to a fine paste.

5 Return the cooled stock to the saucepan and slowly whisk in the chicken mixture, then place over high heat, stirring occasionally. As the stock heats, the chicken and egg white mixture will start to coagulate, rising to the surface to form a layer, or 'raft'. When this happens, turn the heat down to very low to ensure the stock doesn't boil, as boiling will ruin the clarification. Simmer very gently for 10 minutes then carefully make a hole in the centre of the raft, to enable the stock to 'breathe' – make sure the hole is big enough to fit a ladle through, ready for when the time comes to remove the clarified stock. Simmer for 1 hour; during this time, the stock should become crystal clear.

6 Carefully ladle the clarified stock out of the saucepan, taking care not to disturb the raft, as this will cloud the mixture. Strain through a muslin-lined sieve placed over a large saucepan.

7 Meanwhile, blanch each variety of mushrooms in a large pan of boiling salted water for 2 minutes or until softened, then drain well and set aside.

8 Return the consomme in the saucepan to the stove and heat through over low heat.

9 Divide the mixed blanched mushrooms among serving bowls, then spoon over the hot consomme. Drizzle with truffle oil, scatter over the tarragon and top with some black truffle shavings, if using.

CLAM CHOWDER

SERVES 4

This hearty soup is particularly good on a blustery winter evening. Serve it with big chunks of crusty baguette and a fresh green salad.

---

100 ml white wine
1 kg clams
2 sweetcorn, husks and silks removed
25 g butter
1 onion, cut into small dice
1 leek, white part only, well washed, cut into small dice

100 g smoked bacon, cut into small dice
2 stalks celery, cut into small dice
2 cloves garlic, finely chopped
1 potato, cut into small dice
1 fresh bay leaf, torn
600 ml fish stock (see page 223)

2½ tablespoons pouring cream
1 tablespoon flat-leaf parsley, chopped
2 basil leaves, chopped
crusty bread, to serve

---

1 Place a heavy-based saucepan over high heat. Once hot, add the wine and clams to the pan, cover tightly with a lid and cook, shaking the pan occasionally, for 5 minutes or until the clams have opened.

2 Strain the clams, reserving the cooking liquid. When the clams are cool enough to handle, remove them from their shells and set aside. Strain the reserved cooking liquid through a muslin-lined sieve and set aside.

3 Place a corn cob upright on a chopping board and, with a sharp knife, carefully cut downwards along the cob to remove the kernels. Repeat with the remaining cob, transfer the kernels to a bowl and set aside.

4 Melt the butter in a large heavy-based saucepan over medium heat, then add the onion, leek, bacon, celery and garlic and cook, stirring, for 5 minutes, taking care not to let the vegetables colour. Add the potato and corn kernels and cook for a further 2 minutes. Add the bay leaf, fish stock and the reserved cooking liquid and bring to a simmer. Reduce the heat to low then cook for 30 minutes or until the vegetables are tender.

5 Stir in the clams and cream and season to taste with salt and pepper. Sprinkle over the chopped herbs and serve immediately with crusty bread.

PASTA AND GNOCCHI

LINGUINE WITH BABY OCTOPUS, CHILLI AND TARRAGON

SERVES 4

The great thing about this dish is you can prepare the octopus and the sauce in advance, then when your guests arrive, all you need to do is boil the pasta and toss the octopus on the barbecue for a few minutes. Basil stalks are used in the sauce for their intense flavour; save the picked basil leaves to make a fresh pesto for another meal.

1.2 kg baby octopus, cleaned and
    beak removed
⅓ cup (80 ml) olive oil
3 cloves garlic, sliced
1 large red chilli, sliced
1 large green chilli, sliced
pinch of salt

400 g dried linguine
½ bunch tarragon, leaves picked
watercress salad, to serve

TOMATO SAUCE
8 vine-ripened tomatoes
25 ml olive oil

3 golden shallots, finely sliced
2 cloves garlic, finely sliced
½ red chilli, sliced
¼ bunch basil, stalks only
2 tablespoons red wine vinegar
1 teaspoon sugar
salt and pepper

1 Place the octopus in a bowl with the olive oil, garlic, chilli and salt and place in the fridge to marinate for at least 1 hour.

2 Meanwhile, start on the tomato sauce. Use a small, sharp knife to cut a cross in the base of each tomato. Bring plenty of salted water to the boil in a large saucepan, add the tomatoes and blanch for about 30 seconds, then remove with a slotted spoon and transfer to a bowl of iced water. Drain well, then peel the tomatoes and cut into quarters. Remove the seeds and cut the flesh into strips.

3 Heat the olive oil in a heavy-based pan over medium–high heat, then add the shallot and garlic and cook for 2–3 minutes or until the shallot starts to colour. Add the chilli, basil stalks and tomato, reduce the heat to low–medium and cook for 2 minutes. Add the vinegar and sugar, season and cook for 5 minutes or until most of the liquid has evaporated.

4 Cook the pasta in plenty of boiling salted water according to the instructions on the packet, then drain.

5 Remove the octopus from the marinade with a slotted spoon. Preheat a chargrill pan or barbecue to medium–high and cook the octopus for 3–4 minutes, turning occasionally and brushing with the reserved marinade.

6 Remove the basil stalks from the tomato sauce, then toss the sauce, pasta and octopus together and divide among four bowls. Serve with tarragon leaves scattered on top and accompany with a watercress salad.

PUMPKIN TORTELLINI WITH SPICED LENTILS

SERVES 6

There are few things more rewarding than making your own pasta – especially tortellini. Leave yourself plenty of time, put on some inspiring music and throw yourself into it.

200 g green beans, trimmed
salt and pepper
olive oil, for cooking

SPICED LENTILS
½ cup (100 g) red lentils
1 teaspoon coriander seeds
1 teaspoon cumin seeds
6 cardamom pods, seeds removed
3 tablespoons vegetable oil
1 small onion, finely chopped
3 cloves garlic, finely chopped
1 × 4 cm piece ginger, finely chopped
1 × 400 g can chopped tomatoes
1½ cups (375 ml) vegetable stock
   (see page 222)
salt and pepper
lemon juice, to taste

PASTA DOUGH
500 g '00' pasta flour,
   plus extra for dusting
8 egg yolks
3 eggs
2 teaspoons olive oil

PUMPKIN FILLING
2 tablespoons extra virgin olive oil,
   plus extra for tossing
400 g butternut pumpkin (squash),
   peeled, seeded and chopped
   into 1 cm dice
2 bunches cavolo nero (Tuscan kale),
   trimmed and tough stems removed
   (you'll need about 200 g
   trimmed leaves)
20 g butter
1 clove garlic, chopped
400 g fresh ricotta
½ bunch mint, leaves picked
   and finely chopped
½ bunch coriander, leaves picked
   and finely chopped
salt and pepper

CORIANDER YOGHURT
200 g Greek-style yoghurt
1 bunch coriander, leaves picked
   and finely chopped
2½ teaspoons lemon juice

1 First, make the spiced lentils. Wash the lentils until the water runs clear then leave them to soak in fresh water for 3 hours.

2 Grind the spices using a pestle and mortar or an electric spice grinder. Heat the vegetable oil in a saucepan over medium heat, add the spices, onion, garlic and ginger and cook, stirring, for 4–5 minutes or until the onion is light golden.

3 Drain the lentils and add to the onion mixture with the tomatoes and stock. Bring the mixture to the boil, then reduce the heat to low and simmer for 1 hour or until the lentils are very tender and the mixture is quite thick. Season to taste with salt, pepper and a little lemon juice, and set aside until needed.

4 To make the pasta dough, combine the flour, egg yolks, eggs and olive oil in a food processor and process until the mixture resembles fine breadcrumbs. Tip onto a clean benchtop and knead until the dough is smooth and firm. Wrap in plastic film and refrigerate for 30 minutes.

5 For the filling, heat the olive oil in a saucepan over medium heat, add the pumpkin and cook, covered, for 20 minutes or until soft. Remove from the heat and set aside to cool before lightly mashing. Blanch the cavolo nero in boiling salted water for 2 minutes, then drain well. Melt the butter in a saucepan over medium heat, add the garlic and cook, stirring, for 2 minutes or until softened slightly. Add the cavolo nero and cook for another 2 minutes. Drain the mixture well, cool to room temperature then squeeze the cavolo nero to remove as much excess liquid as possible. Finely chop the cavolo nero and combine it with the pumpkin, ricotta and herbs in a bowl. Season to taste and set aside.

6 Divide the chilled pasta dough into three equal pieces and flatten with your hands. Working with one piece at a time (and keeping the others covered with a damp tea towel to prevent them drying out), roll through a pasta machine, starting at the highest setting then working through to the lowest. Very lightly flour the rolled sheet, gently fold, then store under the damp tea towel while you roll the remaining sheets.

7 Using a 7 cm cutter, cut the pasta sheets into 30 rounds. Place a teaspoon of the filling in the centre of each round and brush around the edge with water. Fold the round in half and press gently on the edges to seal, taking care to expel any air bubbles, then join up the ends to form a tortellini shape. Transfer to a large tray or plate lined with non-stick baking paper and cover with plastic film while you make the remaining tortellini.

8 Working in batches, cook the tortellini in plenty of boiling salted water for 2–3 minutes or until cooked through. Drain well, then transfer to a bowl and toss with a little olive oil to prevent them sticking.

9 Blanch the green beans in plenty of boiling salted water for 2–3 minutes, then refresh in cold water, drain and set aside.

10 Warm the spiced lentils over a low heat until heated through.

11 To make the coriander yoghurt, mix together all the ingredients in a small bowl and set aside.

12 To serve, spoon the spiced lentils into pasta bowls and arrange the tortellini and green beans on top. Spoon over the coriander yoghurt to finish.

MACARONI WITH BROAD BEANS AND PANCETTA

SERVES 4

Simple, quick and delicious. For the best results, use the finest pancetta and parmesan you can afford.

---

350 g fresh broad beans (from about
  1 kg beans in pods)
400 g dried short tubular pasta
  such as macaroni or penne

2½ tablespoons olive oil
200 g skinless pancetta,
  cut into strips
2 cloves garlic, sliced

½ bunch mint, leaves picked
2½ tablespoons lemon juice
50 g grated parmesan, or to taste

---

1 Bring plenty of salted water to the boil in a large saucepan, then toss in the broad beans for 1 minute to blanch. Drain and immediately plunge into iced water, then drain again. Remove the tough skins from the larger beans (the skins on the smaller beans are generally more tender but can also be removed if you wish).

2 Cook the pasta in plenty of boiling salted water according to the instructions on the packet then drain well.

3 Meanwhile, heat the oil in a heavy-based frying pan over medium heat, then add the pancetta and cook, stirring, for 2–3 minutes or until brown and crisp. Add the garlic and cook for a further minute, then add the broad beans, drained pasta and mint. Toss together and cook for another minute or until heated through. Drizzle over the lemon juice and serve immediately with plenty of grated parmesan.

LINGUINE WITH MUSSELS AND PEAS

SERVES 6

This delicious pasta is perfect served as a main, or do as the Italians do and enjoy it as an appetiser, followed with a meat dish as a second course. Buy the mussels on the day you will be serving them. When cooking mussels, my tip is not to throw out any stubborn ones that do not open. Despite what many people think, they are not off – often they just need a little extra cooking time. (Of course, discard them if they don't smell quite right.)

---

2 slices (about 150 g) rustic bread
   such as sourdough, crusts removed,
   bread torn into small pieces
½ cup (125 ml) extra virgin olive oil
2 onions, sliced
5 cloves garlic, 2 crushed,
   3 chopped

2 bay leaves
4 sprigs thyme
2 kg mussels, scrubbed and debearded
300 ml white wine
300 g fresh peas (from about
   600 g peas in pods)
150 g butter

1 large red chilli, chopped
handful flat-leaf parsley leaves,
   coarsely chopped
500 g dried linguine
salt and pepper

---

1 Preheat the oven to 180°C.

2 Place the bread on an oven tray and drizzle over ⅓ cup (80 ml) of the oil, tossing to coat well. Bake in the oven for 3–5 minutes or until golden and crisp, then set aside.

3 Heat the remaining oil in a large heavy-based saucepan over high heat, add the onions, crushed garlic and herbs and cook, stirring, for 1–2 minutes. Add the mussels and wine, cover and shake the pan. Cook for 2–3 minutes, shaking the pan occasionally, until the mussels start to open. Remove the pan from the heat and, when cool enough to handle, fish out the mussels and remove them from their shells (though you can leave some in their shells if you like, to make the final dish look even more impressive). Strain the cooking liquid through a muslin-lined sieve and reserve.

4 Bring a small saucepan of water to the boil, add the peas and cook for 3 minutes or until tender, then drain. Plunge the peas into a bowl of iced water to cool, then drain again and set aside.

5 Heat half the butter in a large heavy-based saucepan over medium heat, add the chilli and chopped garlic and cook, stirring, for 30 seconds. Add the reserved cooking stock, bring to the boil then cook for 8–10 minutes or until the liquid has reduced by half. Add the remaining butter, the peas and the chopped parsley to the pan, swirling to combine well.

6 Meanwhile, cook the pasta in plenty of boiling salted water according to the instructions on the packet, then drain well.

7 Add the drained pasta and the mussels to the pea mixture, toss to combine well and season with salt and pepper. Divide among warmed bowls, sprinkle over the breadcrumbs then serve immediately.

SILVERBEET ROTOLO WITH CHILLI AND LEMON

SERVES 6

Rotolo is the Italian word for 'roll'. This is a great dish for vegetarians – all it needs is a fresh green salad to accompany it. You could also serve the sage and pine nut sauce with fresh pumpkin ravioli.

PASTA DOUGH
1⅔ cups (250 g) 'OO' pasta flour
1 egg
4 egg yolks
1 teaspoon salt
1 teaspoon olive oil

SILVERBEET FILLING
1 bunch silverbeet (Swiss chard)
1½ tablespoons lemon juice,
　　plus extra to serve
20 g butter
1 brown onion, finely chopped
2 cloves garlic, finely chopped
1 red chilli, finely chopped
salt and pepper
¼ teaspoon ground nutmeg
1 cup (240 g) firm fresh ricotta

2 tablespoons grated parmesan
2 teaspoons finely grated lemon zest

SAGE AND PINE NUT SAUCE
80 g butter
½ large red chilli, finely sliced
½ bunch sage, leaves picked
1 tablespoon pine nuts, toasted
2 teaspoons chopped lemon flesh

1 To prepare the pasta dough, place all the ingredients in a food processor and process until the mixture resembles fine breadcrumbs. Tip out onto a clean benchtop and knead until a firm, smooth dough forms. Wrap in plastic film and leave to rest for 30 minutes.

2 To prepare the filling, cut the green leaves away from the stalks and tough ribs of the silverbeet, retaining the stalks. Wash the leaves well, shake dry, then roughly chop and set aside. Cut the stalks into sticks about 2.5 cm long and 5 mm wide. Bring a saucepan of salted water to the boil, add the lemon juice then cook the stalks for 2–3 minutes or until tender. Drain well, then plunge into iced water to refresh. Drain again and set aside.

3 Melt the butter in a large saucepan over medium heat, add the onion, garlic and chilli and cook, stirring often, for 2 minutes or until softened. Add the chopped silverbeet leaves to the pan, season with salt, pepper and nutmeg and cook, stirring often, for 3–4 minutes or until the leaves are tender and all the moisture has evaporated. Remove from the heat and leave to cool. Once cold, add the ricotta, parmesan and lemon zest and mix together well.

4 On a lightly floured benchtop, roll out the pasta with a rolling pin to a thickness of 2 mm. Trim the sides to form a 20 cm × 40 cm rectangle. Spread the silverbeet mixture over the pasta, leaving a 2 cm border around the edges, and then roll up like a Swiss roll.

5 Bring a large saucepan of water fitted with a steamer insert to the boil. Carefully transfer the rotolo to the steamer, then cover and cook for 20 minutes.

6 Meanwhile, to prepare the sauce, melt the butter in a small saucepan over medium heat until it foams and turns a nutty brown colour. Remove from the heat, then stir in the chilli, sage leaves, pine nuts, lemon and the reserved blanched silverbeet stalks.

7 Remove the rotolo from the steamer, place on a board and cut into six even pieces. Place on serving plates, spoon over the sauce and add a final squeeze of lemon juice to taste before serving.

GNOCCHI WITH OXTAIL

SERVES 6

A bit of time and effort is required here, but it is well worth it. Both the gnocchi and the braise can be made in advance and stored in the fridge (the flavours of the braise will improve over time anyway). Gnocchi can be a bit tricky, largely because of the variable moisture content of potatoes. Roasting the potatoes on a bed of rock salt really helps to draw out the moisture, and produces a much lighter gnocchi.

3 vine-ripened tomatoes
½ cup (125 ml) olive oil
2.5 kg oxtail, cut into slices (ask your butcher to do this for you)
2 carrots, coarsely chopped
2 onions, coarsely chopped
3 stalks celery, coarsely chopped
4 cloves garlic, crushed
2 cups (500 ml) red wine

1 litre veal jus (see page 225)
2 cups (500 ml) chicken stock (see page 222)
1 teaspoon white peppercorns
2 carrots, cut into 1 cm dice
1 head celeriac, peeled and cut into 1 cm dice
¼ bunch flat-leaf parsley, chopped
50 g grated parmesan, or to taste

GNOCCHI
2 cups (600 g) rock salt
1 kg pontiac potatoes
100 g plain flour
1 egg yolk
salt, to taste
100 g cultured unsalted butter, chopped

1 To make the gnocchi, preheat the oven to 180°C and spread the rock salt over a baking tray. Place the whole, unpeeled potatoes on the salt and bake for 1–1½ hours or until tender. Leave to cool slightly, then cut in half and scoop out the flesh. Push the flesh through a potato ricer into a bowl and leave to cool. Add the flour, egg yolk and salt and mix together until a soft dough forms.

2 Divide the dough into eight equal portions. Working with one piece at a time (and keeping the others covered with a damp tea towel), roll out on a lightly floured benchtop into a log about 2 cm wide. Cut the logs into 2 cm pieces.

3 Bring a large saucepan of salted water to the boil and cook the gnocchi in batches for 2–3 minutes or until they rise to the surface. Remove to a tray or large plate using a slotted spoon, draining the gnocchi well. You can make the gnocchi to this stage up to 24 hours ahead of time and store covered in the refrigerator.

4 To make the sauce, preheat the oven to 160°C.

5 Use a small, sharp knife to cut a cross in the base of each tomato. Bring plenty of salted water to the boil in a large saucepan. Add the tomatoes and blanch for about 30 seconds, then remove with a slotted spoon and transfer to a bowl of iced water. Drain well, then peel the tomatoes and cut into quarters. Remove the seeds and cut the flesh into dice. Set aside.

6 Heat 2 tablespoons of the oil in a large heavy-based frying pan over medium heat. Add half the oxtail and cook for 6–7 minutes or until browned all over, turning often. Transfer to a large casserole. Repeat with another 2 tablespoons oil and the remaining oxtail. Heat half the remaining oil in the pan, add half the vegetables and cook, stirring often, for 7–8 minutes or until golden. Transfer to the casserole, then repeat with the remaining oil and vegetables. Add the red wine to the frying pan, place over high heat and boil for 3 minutes or until reduced slightly, stirring to dislodge any stuck-on bits. Add this to the casserole along with the jus, stock and peppercorns. Bring the mixture to a simmer over medium heat, then cover tightly and transfer to the oven. Cook for 4 hours or until the meat is falling off the bone.

7 Once cooked, remove the oxtail with a slotted spoon and set aside until cool enough to handle. Strain the cooking liquid into a large saucepan, discarding the vegetables. Remove the meat from the bones, discarding them and any gristle, then coarsely shred the meat. Skim the fat from the surface of the cooking liquid then bring to the boil over high heat. Reduce the heat to medium and simmer for 20 minutes or until thickened slightly.

8 Cook the diced carrot and celeriac in boiling salted water for 5–6 minutes or until tender, then drain well. Add the carrot, celeriac, chopped tomato and shredded meat to the sauce in the pan and cook over medium heat for 5 minutes or until heated through. Stir in the parsley just before serving.

9 To serve, melt the butter in a large frying pan. Add the gnocchi and cook, tossing, for 2 minutes or until heated through. Divide among six bowls, then spoon the oxtail sauce over and scatter with freshly grated parmesan.

BRAISED RABBIT WITH WHITE WINE, PEAS AND PAPPARDELLE

SERVES 4

I love to dish up this sort of comfort food for friends on a cold, wintry evening. You can make the rich, delicious rabbit sauce in advance and keep it warm, then, as your guests arrive and enjoy a drink, cook the peas and pasta and you are ready to go.

100 ml olive oil
1 carrot, chopped
1 red onion, chopped
1 stalk celery, chopped
2 sprigs rosemary
1 bay leaf
3 cloves garlic, crushed

salt and pepper
150 ml white wine
1 × 1.4 kg farmed rabbit, cut into legs, shoulders and loins (ask your butcher to do this for you)
1.5 litres chicken stock (see page 222)
1 red chilli, deseeded and finely sliced

30 g butter
1¼ cups (200 g) fresh peas (from about 400 g peas in pods)
500 g dried pappardelle
½ bunch mint, leaves picked

1 Preheat the oven to 150°C.

2 Heat half the oil in a casserole over medium heat and when hot, add the carrot, onion, celery, rosemary, bay leaf and garlic. Season lightly with salt and pepper then cook, stirring often, for 15 minutes or until the vegetables have softened and are light golden. Add the white wine, bring to the boil, then cook for about 8 minutes over high heat or until the wine has reduced to a syrupy consistency.

3 Meanwhile, heat the remaining oil in a heavy-based frying pan over medium–high heat. Season the rabbit with salt and pepper then place in the hot pan. Cook, turning occasionally, for approximately 5–6 minutes or until browned all over.

4 Add the browned rabbit to the casserole then pour over the chicken stock. Bring to a simmer, then place a piece of greaseproof paper on top of the liquid and cover the casserole with the lid. Braise in the oven for 2½ hours or until the rabbit is cooked and tender.

5 When the rabbit is cool enough to handle, remove it from the cooking liquid and carefully pick the meat from the bones, discarding the bones.

6 Strain the cooking liquid into a saucepan, discarding the vegetables. Simmer over a medium–high heat for 10 minutes or until the liquid has reduced by about two-thirds, then add the chilli and whisk in the butter. Add the rabbit meat to the sauce and keep warm.

7 Bring plenty of salted water to the boil in a large saucepan then toss in the peas for 1 minute to blanch. Remove and transfer to the rabbit sauce.

8 Meanwhile, cook the pasta in plenty of boiling salted water according to the instructions on the packet, then drain well.

9 Stir the rabbit sauce and the mint through the pasta, toss to combine well and serve immediately.

TORTELLINI WITH SPINACH, RICOTTA, FENNEL AND ORANGE

SERVES 6

You could use different leaves with this recipe, such as chicory or rocket. The candied orange zest adds an amazing citrussy punch, and works well in both savoury and sweet dishes (though you might like to try the version on page 214 to use with sweet dishes).

125 g butter
juice of 1 lemon
2 oranges, peeled and cut into segments
1 bulb baby fennel, trimmed and
    finely sliced, fronds reserved
30 g pine nuts, toasted
1 small handful radicchio leaves
1 small handful red coral leaves
1 small handful frisee
    (curly endive) leaves
60 g parmesan, shaved

PASTA DOUGH
500 g 'OO' pasta flour
8 egg yolks
3 whole eggs
2 teaspoons olive oil
pinch of salt

SPINACH AND RICOTTA FILLING
olive oil, for cooking
1 bunch English spinach, washed and
    trimmed, leaves roughly chopped

20 g pine nuts, toasted
pinch of nutmeg
salt and pepper
65 g fresh ricotta
finely grated zest of ½ lemon

CANDIED ORANGE ZEST
75 g sugar
75 ml rice wine vinegar
1 Valencia orange, zest removed
    in strips with a vegetable peeler

---

1 To prepare the candied orange zest, first make a sugar syrup. Place the sugar and rice wine vinegar in a small saucepan over low heat and stir until the sugar has dissolved. Remove from the heat and allow to cool.

2 Blanch the orange zest in a saucepan of boiling water for 1–2 minutes. Remove and refresh in a bowl of iced water, then transfer to the saucepan with the sugar syrup.

3 Return this to the stove and bring to the boil, reduce the heat to low and cook for 10–15 minutes until the zest is tender. Leave to cool then slice very thinly and set aside.

4 To make the pasta dough, combine the flour, egg yolks, eggs, olive oil and salt in a food processor until the mixture resembles fine breadcrumbs. Tip onto a clean benchtop and knead until the dough is smooth and firm. Wrap in plastic film and refrigerate for 30 minutes.

5 To make the filling, heat a little olive oil in a large frying pan over medium heat. Add the spinach, pine nuts and nutmeg and cook for a minute or so until the spinach is wilted. Season to taste with salt and pepper and set aside to cool, then fold in the ricotta and lemon zest.

6 Divide the chilled dough into three equal pieces and flatten with your hands. Working with one piece at a time (and keeping the others covered with a damp tea towel to prevent them drying out), roll through a pasta machine, starting at the highest setting then working through to the lowest. Very lightly flour the rolled sheet, gently fold, then store under the damp tea towel while you roll the remaining sheets.

7 Using a 7 cm cutter, cut the pasta sheets into 30 rounds. Place a teaspoon of the filling in the centre of each pasta round and brush around the edge with water. Fold the round in half and press gently on the edges to seal, taking care to expel any air bubbles, then join up the ends to form a tortellini shape. Transfer to a large tray or plate lined with non-stick baking paper and cover with plastic film while you make the remaining tortellini. Working in batches, cook the tortellini in plenty of boiling salted water for 2–3 minutes or until cooked through. Drain well, transfer to a bowl and toss through a little olive oil to prevent them sticking.

8 Meanwhile, melt the butter in a small saucepan over high heat and cook for 1–2 minutes or until it turns a nutty-brown colour. Stir in the lemon juice.

9 Divide the cooked tortellini among serving plates and decorate the plate with the orange segments, fennel, fennel fronds, pine nuts, salad leaves, shaved parmesan and candied zest. Spoon the lemon butter over and serve.

SEAFOOD

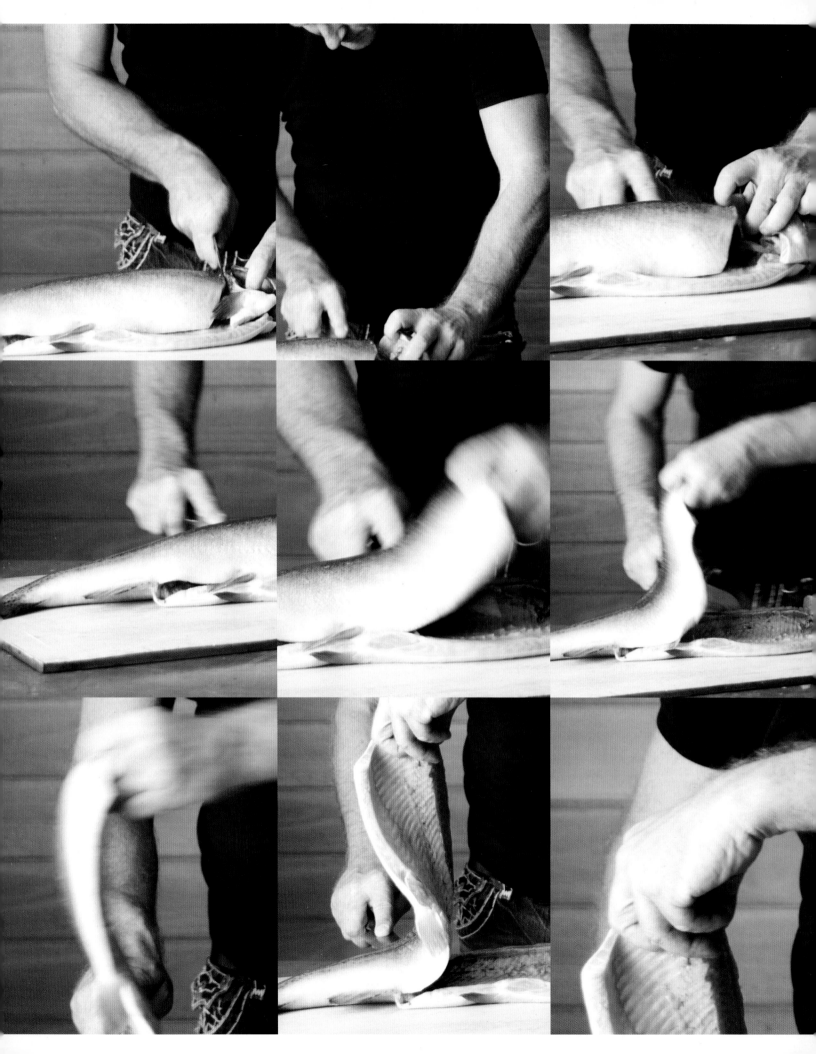

SCALLOPS WITH BRUSSELS SPROUTS

SERVES 6 AS A STARTER

This very elegant appetiser is best served in winter, when Brussels sprouts are readily available. None of the components is hard to make – each just takes a little time. You can store the spiced salt in an airtight container and use it for seasoning all sorts of meat and fish dishes.

450 g Brussels sprouts,
   3 left whole, the
   rest cut into very fine shreds
50 g grated parmesan
¼ cup (60 ml) extra virgin olive oil
2 tablespoons white balsamic vinegar
salt and pepper
1½ tablespoons chopped chives
2 tablespoons vegetable oil
18 scallops

PUMPKIN PUREE
25 g butter
250 g Queensland blue pumpkin,
   peeled, seeded and cut into
   2 cm pieces
½ small clove garlic
½ sprig thyme
1¼ tablespoons chicken stock
   (see page 222), optional
salt and pepper

CAPER AND RAISIN PUREE
125 g raisins
1½ cups (375 ml) verjuice
85 g capers, rinsed

SPICED SALT
2 blades mace
2 teaspoons cumin seeds
1 teaspoon ground turmeric
1 tablespoon salt

1 For the pumpkin puree, melt the butter in a large saucepan over low–medium heat. Add the pumpkin, garlic and thyme, cover and cook, stirring occasionally, for 10 minutes or until the pumpkin is very soft. Transfer to a food processor or blender and process to a smooth puree, adding a little chicken stock or water as needed to make a soft consistency that will drop off the spoon. Season to taste.

2 For the caper and raisin puree, combine the raisins with the verjuice in a small saucepan, bring to a simmer then cover the pan and remove from the heat. Leave to stand for 1 hour, then strain off the liquid and transfer the raisins to a food processor. Add the capers and blend until smooth. Push the mixture through a fine-meshed sieve and set aside.

3 To make the spiced salt, firstly combine the mace and cumin seeds in an electric spice grinder or a mortar and pestle and grind to a fine powder, then stir through the turmeric and salt. Spoon out 2 teaspoons of the mixture into a small bowl and store the remainder in an airtight container for another use.

4 Combine the shredded Brussels sprouts in a bowl with the parmesan, olive oil and vinegar and season to taste. Add the chives, toss to combine, then set aside.

5 Bring a small saucepan of salted water to the boil. Carefully remove as many of the leaves intact from the reserved sprouts as possible, then blanch the whole leaves for 1–2 minutes or until just tender. Drain well, then refresh in iced water and drain again before setting them aside.

6 Heat the oil in a large frying pan over medium–high heat. Sprinkle one side of the scallops with some spiced salt, then place them, salt-side down, in the pan and cook for 2–3 minutes or until deep golden. Turn the scallops over then immediately remove them from the pan.

7 To serve, place a dollop of pumpkin puree on each plate and smear it with the back of a spoon. Dot some caper and raisin puree around the plate, then arrange the shredded Brussels sprouts in three small piles. Place a scallop on each, and scatter the blanched leaves alongside.

GRILLED PRAWNS WITH CAULIFLOWER AND WHITE MISO DRESSING

SERVES 6 AS A STARTER

This is an unusual combination of flavours that works really well. I think cauliflower is greatly underrated, and I love this puree. You could easily make more and serve it with a meat dish.

½ small cauliflower, trimmed and cut
    into florets (you'll need about 300 g)
2 tablespoons vegetable oil
12 green jumbo king prawns, peeled
    and deveined, with tails intact
100 g butter
100 g baby spinach
salt and pepper
¼ granny smith apple, cored and
    very finely sliced
50 g slivered almonds, toasted
small handful of baby coriander or
    regular coriander

CAULIFLOWER PUREE
40 g butter
½ small cauliflower, trimmed
    and finely chopped
    (you'll need about 300 g)
½ cup (125 ml) pouring cream
salt and pepper

WHITE MISO DRESSING
100 g white miso
½ small golden shallot,
    chopped
1 cm piece ginger, chopped
½ red chilli, chopped
1½ tablespoons lemon juice
1 tablespoon mirin
1 teaspoon rice wine
2 teaspoons tahini
1 tablespoon honey
1 tablespoon caster sugar
1¼ tablespoons grapeseed oil

1 To make the cauliflower puree, heat the butter in a small saucepan over low heat. Add the cauliflower, then cover and cook, stirring occasionally, for 10–15 minutes or until the cauliflower is very soft but not coloured. Add a few teaspoons of water if the cauliflower starts to stick. Stir in the cream, then transfer to a food processor or blender and process to a smooth puree. Season to taste, then set aside. Gently reheat just before serving if necessary.

2 For the white miso dressing, place all the ingredients in a food processor or blender along with 75 ml water and blend until smooth. Push through a fine-meshed sieve and set aside.

3 Cook the cauliflower in boiling, salted water for 4 minutes or until just tender. Drain well and set aside.

4 Preheat a chargrill plate over medium–high heat. Combine the vegetable oil and prawns in a bowl and toss to coat. Add the prawns to the chargrill, in batches if necessary, and cook for about 3 minutes or until just cooked through, turning once.

5 Meanwhile, heat half the butter in a large frying pan over medium heat, add the blanched cauliflower florets and cook, tossing the pan, for 4–5 minutes or until golden. Remove from the pan and set aside. Add the remaining butter to the pan, toss in the baby spinach and cook for 1–2 minutes or until just wilted. Season to taste.

6 To serve, divide the cauliflower puree between six plates. Arrange two prawns on top, followed by the spinach, cauliflower florets and apple. Scatter over the almonds and drizzle with the dressing, then garnish with coriander.

BLUE SWIMMER CRAB WITH BLACK PEPPERCORNS

SERVES 6–8 AS A STARTER

This dish, with its strong Asian influence, is a big hit at dinner parties – just make sure you have plenty of table napkins and bowls of water ready as your guests dig in, bare hands and all. In Australia, this is best served between January and March, when blue swimmer crabs are at their peak.

---

2 whole blue swimmer crabs
½ cup (125 ml) vegetable oil
2 tablespoons black peppercorns
1 red chilli, sliced
4 cloves garlic, sliced

6 spring onions, trimmed and thinly
    sliced on the diagonal
50 g butter
⅓ cup (80 ml) soy sauce
2 tablespoons oyster sauce

1 teaspoon caster sugar
1 bunch coriander, leaves picked
lemon and lime wedges, to serve

---

1 Working with one crab at a time, hold the crab upside down, lift the tail flaps and lift off the upper shell. Remove and discard the grey gills (dead man's fingers) and the orange coral (mustard). Using a large sharp knife, cut each crab body into four pieces. Using the back of the knife, firmly tap on the claws to crack the shells, but leave the claws intact.

2 Heat the vegetable oil in a wok or large frying pan over high heat until smoking, then add the crab pieces and stir-fry for 2–3 minutes. Remove with a slotted spoon and set aside.

3 Add the black peppercorns, chilli, garlic, spring onions and butter to the pan and cook for 1 minute. Stir in the soy sauce, oyster sauce, sugar and 300 ml water and return the crab pieces to the pan. Bring to the boil then simmer for 7–8 minutes or until the sauce thickens and coats the crab.

4 Arrange the crab pieces on a large plate and spoon over the sauce. Scatter over the coriander and serve with lemon and lime wedges to squeeze over.

SWORDFISH WITH YUZU PUREE AND PICKLED RADISH SALAD

SERVES 6 AS A STARTER

This Japanese-inspired recipe uses a few interesting ingredients. Bonito flakes are thin shavings of dried, smoked bonito fish. Perilla, also known as shiso or Japanese basil, is an aromatic herb with a purple or green leaf. Yuzu juice comes from a Japanese citrus fruit that tastes somewhere between a lemon and a lime but is less acidic than either. All three should be available from an Asian or Japanese grocer. Ask your fishmonger to trim and roll the swordfish for you.

1½ tablespoons light soy sauce
100 ml rice wine vinegar
¼ cup (4 g) bonito flakes
¼ cup (60 ml) vegetable oil
2 × 400 g pieces sashimi-grade
  swordfish, trimmed of bloodline
  and rolled (ask your fishmonger
  to do this for you)
2 sprigs perilla
small handful frisee
  (curly endive) leaves
1 spring onion, green part only, sliced
  very thinly on the diagonal

PICKLED DAIKON
3 teaspoons light soy sauce
70 g caster sugar
150 ml rice wine vinegar
1 × 300 g piece daikon, peeled and
  sliced into 2 mm thick rounds

PICKLED RED RADISH
120 ml rice wine vinegar
⅓ cup (75 g) caster sugar
½ teaspoon salt
5 red radishes, trimmed,
  leaving about ½ cm stalk remaining

YUZU PUREE
1 cup (250 ml) yuzu juice
⅓ cup (75 g) caster sugar
25 ml rice wine vinegar
5 g agar agar

1 To make the pickled daikon, combine the soy sauce, sugar, vinegar and 300 ml water in a small saucepan, then bring to a simmer over medium heat, stirring to dissolve the sugar. Add the daikon and simmer for 1 minute, then remove the pan from the heat and leave the daikon to cool in the liquid (it will continue to cook slowly as it cools).

2 For the pickled red radish, combine the vinegar, sugar, salt and 225 ml water in a small saucepan, bring to a simmer over medium heat and cook for 1 minute, stirring to dissolve the sugar. Add the radishes and cook for 2 minutes, then remove the pan from the heat and leave the radishes to cool in the liquid (they will continue to cook slowly as they cool). Cut the radishes into quarters and transfer to a bowl.

3 To make the yuzu puree, place the yuzu juice, sugar, vinegar and 75 ml water in a saucepan over medium heat. Whisk in the agar agar and bring to the boil, whisking continuously. Boil for 1 minute, then strain the mixture into a bowl and transfer to the refrigerator to set (this should take 1–2 hours).

4 Once the mixture has set, spoon into a food processor and process to a puree, then strain through a fine-meshed sieve. Transfer to a piping bag or plastic squeezy bottle.

5 Place the light soy sauce, vinegar and bonito flakes in a small saucepan and bring to the boil. Cook for 1 minute, then remove the pan from the heat and allow to cool. Once cooled, strain through a fine-meshed sieve to make a smooth glaze and set aside.

6 In a frying pan, heat the vegetable oil then briefly seal the swordfish pieces on all sides. Remove to a chopping board and cut into 1 cm thick slices.

7 To serve, place three rounds of daikon on each plate and top with three slices of the sealed swordfish. Brush the swordfish with the soy glaze, squeeze dots of yuzu puree around the fish, then arrange the pickled radish, perilla, frisee and spring onion alongside.

SEAFOOD BANQUET

SERVES 6–8

Nothing says summer in Australia quite like a seafood banquet. This is a great menu to serve for a celebration lunch or dinner – perhaps as a refreshing alternative to the traditional Christmas Day fare, or as a lovely feast for close friends on New Year's Eve. Take the time to make a special trip to the fish markets on the day that you are entertaining, so that your seafood will be ocean-fresh, and serve the salad, swordfish and prawns together, banquet-style. Wash it all down with some crisp white wine.

RUSTIC BISTRO MENU

SERVES 6

This menu is reminiscent of the wholesome food that you could expect to eat in a small bistro in the French countryside. Rillettes can be found in every charcuterie in France, and these ones make a very tasty starter. Chicken fricassee is comfort food at its finest, and the fig kouing-aman is an irresistible dish that complements the other courses perfectly.

BBQ PRAWNS WITH NAM JIM DRESSING

SERVES 4 AS A STARTER OR LIGHT MEAL

This dish is great for a summer barbecue under the stars, and the nam jim dressing gives it a distinctly Asian flavour. Galangal comes from the same family as ginger, and has a similar but stronger flavour. It is available from Asian grocers and specialty stores.

½ large cucumber, thinly sliced
½ bulb fennel, trimmed and thinly sliced, fronds reserved
1 spring onion, trimmed and thinly sliced
½ large red chilli, very finely sliced lengthways

small handful mint leaves
small handful coriander leaves
12 large raw king prawns, peeled and deveined, with tails intact
1 tablespoon vegetable oil
salt and pepper
lime halves, to garnish

NAM JIM DRESSING
1 clove garlic, chopped
½ bunch coriander, leaves picked and chopped
1 large green chilli, seeded and chopped
4 teaspoons chopped galangal
2 tablespoons shaved palm sugar
2 tablespoons fish sauce
2 tablespoons lime juice
⅔ cup (160 ml) vegetable oil

1 For the nam jim dressing, combine all the ingredients in a food processor or blender and process until smooth then set aside.

2 Combine the cucumber, fennel, fennel fronds, spring onion and chilli in a bowl, then add the herbs and toss together gently.

3 In a large bowl, toss the prawns with the vegetable oil to coat then season with salt and pepper.

4 Preheat the barbecue to its hottest setting or a chargrill plate over high heat. Grill the prawns for 3 minutes or until just cooked through, turning once. Remove from the heat, transfer to a large platter and season with pepper.

5 Divide the salad among individual bowls and place on the table. Serve the prawns with lime halves to squeeze over, and the nam jim dressing on the side.

SPICED MACKEREL WITH DILL YOGHURT

SERVES 4

You'll need to start making this dish the day before you want to serve it, so the mackerel can marinate in the fridge overnight. The combination of spices gives the dish a really tasty Indian flavour, and you could easily serve it as one of a selection.

1 teaspoon cumin seeds
½ teaspoon coriander seeds
1 teaspoon fennel seeds
1 cinnamon stick
1 teaspoon sea salt
1 teaspoon black peppercorns
3 cloves garlic, finely chopped

1 red chilli, finely chopped
150 g tamarind paste
100 ml vegetable oil
4 whole slippery mackerel, cleaned
watercress to garnish, optional
lemon wedges, to serve

DILL YOGHURT
1 bunch dill, finely chopped
¾ cup (200 g) Greek-style yoghurt
1 tablespoon olive oil

1 To prepare the mackerel, combine the cumin, coriander, fennel and cinnamon in a heavy-based frying pan, place over low–medium heat and dry-fry for about 3 minutes or until fragrant, then remove the pan from the heat and set aside to cool.

2 Transfer the spices to a mortar and pestle, add the salt and peppercorns and grind to a powder. Add the garlic, chilli and tamarind paste then continue to grind until a thick paste forms. Stir in the vegetable oil then set aside.

3 Using a sharp knife, score the mackerel across the skin several times on both sides of the fish, then rub the spice mixture all over the fish and into the cuts. Place the mackerel in the refrigerator and leave to marinate for 24 hours.

4 Preheat the oven to 200°C.

5 To prepare the dill yoghurt, place all the ingredients into a bowl and mix together.

6 Place the mackerel on a baking tray and bake for 15 minutes.

7 Serve the mackerel immediately, garnished with watercress, if using. Serve the dill yoghurt and lemon wedges separately alongside.

SMOKED TROUT WITH BEETROOT RELISH AND HORSERADISH CREME FRAICHE

SERVES 4 AS A LIGHT MEAL

This classic combination is always a big hit. The trout has a delicious, gentle flavour, and the horseradish adds a bit of bite. You could also serve the beetroot relish with cold meats. Apres tea is a special blend made up of different combinations of flavours: the one I used included chamomile, fennel, aniseed and spearmint.

4 rainbow trout fillets, pin-boned
⅓ cup (100 g) rock salt or coarse
    cooking salt
2 teaspoons Earl Grey tea
2 teaspoons English Breakfast tea
2 teaspoons chamomile tea
2 teaspoons apres tea
2 tablespoons jasmine rice
1½ tablespoons caster sugar
1½ tablespoons firmly packed
    brown sugar
small handful rocket leaves
1 tablespoon olive oil

BEETROOT RELISH
250 g beetroot, peeled and grated
100 ml red wine vinegar
3 tablespoons firmly packed
    brown sugar
salt and pepper

HORSERADISH CREME FRAICHE
2 tablespoons creme fraiche
2 teaspoons finely grated horseradish
    or good-quality horseradish sauce
2 teaspoons chopped dill
salt and pepper

1 For the beetroot relish, place all the ingredients along with 100 ml water in a small saucepan. Bring to the boil, cover and reduce the heat to low then cook, stirring occasionally, for 50–60 minutes or until reduced to a jam-like consistency. Season to taste and set aside to cool.

2 For the horseradish creme fraiche, mix together all the ingredients and season to taste with salt and pepper.

3 Place the trout fillets in a ceramic dish and sprinkle both sides with the salt. Cover and refrigerate for 20 minutes.

4 Wash the salt off the fish then pat dry with paper towel. Cut each fillet widthways into three even pieces.

5 In a bowl, mix together the teas, rice and sugars.

6 Line a large saucepan or wok with a couple of layers of foil then warm over medium heat. Place a small heatproof bowl or cup (approximately 8 cm high) upside down in the saucepan. Sprinkle the tea mixture evenly over the base of the saucepan. Once the mixture starts to smoke, place the trout fillets on a rack that will fit in the saucepan, then sit the rack on the bowl or cup in the pan. Increase the heat to high, cover with foil or a tight-fitting lid and leave to smoke for 2 minutes. Carefully remove the rack from the pan and leave the trout to cool.

7 To serve, divide the smoked trout among four plates and add a spoonful of beetroot relish. Dress the rocket leaves with the olive oil and add to the plate, then serve with the horseradish creme fraiche.

PRAWNS WITH ROMESCO SAUCE

SERVES 4

Spanish romesco sauce is great with seafood, but works equally well as a pasta sauce or a dip for fresh vegetables. I like to use piquillo peppers from northern Spain, which have a lovely sweet flavour and are not too hot. They're available from specialty grocers.

12 jumbo green king prawns,
    peeled and deveined, with heads
    and tails intact
2 tablespoons olive oil
salt and pepper
lime cheeks, to serve

ROMESCO SAUCE
2 vine-ripened tomatoes
1½ tablespoons olive oil
1 clove garlic, chopped
½ large red chilli, chopped
1 sprig rosemary
150 g piquillo peppers, chopped

salt and pepper
1 tablespoon lemon juice
2 tablespoons rice wine vinegar
30 g whole blanched almonds,
    lightly toasted

1 To prepare the romesco sauce, use a small, sharp knife to cut a cross in the base of each tomato. Bring plenty of salted water to the boil in a large saucepan. Add the tomatoes and blanch for about 30 seconds, then remove with a slotted spoon and transfer to a bowl of iced water. Drain well, then peel the tomatoes and cut into quarters. Remove the seeds and roughly chop the flesh.

2 Heat the olive oil in a small saucepan over medium heat, add the garlic, chilli and rosemary and cook, stirring, for 1 minute. Increase the heat to high, add the chopped tomato and peppers and season with salt and pepper. Cook, stirring, for 2 minutes, then remove the rosemary sprig and transfer the mixture to a food processor or blender. Add the lemon juice, vinegar and almonds and blend until smooth, then set aside.

3 Heat the grill to its highest setting. Place the prawns on a baking tray, drizzle with olive oil and season with salt and pepper, then cook under the grill for 3 minutes, turning once.

4 To serve, place the prawns on a plate with the lime cheeks and romesco sauce on the side.

STEAMED SALMON WITH WITLOF CHOUCROUTE AND LEMON SAUCE

SERVES 6

This is one of my favourite seafood dishes. The creamy lemon sauce is quite rich, so you don't need all that much, but it goes beautifully with the slightly bitter taste of the witlof. Choucroute is just French for sauerkraut. Chardonnay vinegar is a Spanish white wine vinegar, available from specialty grocers. If you can't get it, use any other good-quality white wine vinegar instead.

1 bunch radishes, well washed and
   trimmed leaving about 1 cm stalk,
   then halved lengthways
300 g small squid, cleaned and scored
2½ tablespoons extra virgin olive oil
1½ tablespoons snipped chives
salt and pepper
6 × 180 g salmon fillets, pin-boned
small handful watercress, leaves picked
mixed salad leaves, to serve

WITLOF CHOUCROUTE
1 star anise
5 × 1.5 cm wide pieces orange zest,
   removed with a vegetable peeler
1½ teaspoons juniper berries,
   lightly crushed
75 g butter
6 witlof (chicory), trimmed and finely
   sliced widthways
2 cloves garlic, chopped
salt and pepper
400 ml white wine
½ cup (125 ml) chardonnay vinegar

LEMON SAUCE
25 g butter
2 golden shallots, thinly sliced
2 cloves garlic, crushed
50 g button mushrooms, sliced
1 sprig thyme
1 bay leaf
25 ml dry vermouth (I like to use
   Noilly Prat)
1 cup (250 ml) fish stock (see page 223)
150 ml pouring cream
salt and pepper
1 sprig tarragon, leaves chopped
1 tablespoon lemon juice,
   plus extra if needed

1 For the witlof choucroute, place the star anise, orange zest and crushed juniper berries in a muslin bag and tie with kitchen string.

2 Melt the butter in a large, heavy-based saucepan over medium heat, then add the witlof, garlic and the spice bag. Season and cook, stirring, for 5 minutes. Add the wine and vinegar and cook for 10 minutes or until all the liquid has been absorbed, then remove from the heat and keep warm.

3 For the lemon sauce, melt the butter in a saucepan, add the shallot and garlic and cook over low–medium heat, stirring often, for 5 minutes or until the shallot is soft but not coloured. Add the mushrooms, thyme and bay leaf and cook for 4–5 minutes. Increase the heat to medium–high, add the dry vermouth and bring to a simmer, cooking for 2–3 minutes or until the liquid is reduced and syrupy. Add the fish stock, bring to a simmer again and cook for 5–6 minutes or until the liquid has reduced by half. Add the cream, bring to a simmer and cook for 10 minutes over medium heat or until reduced and thickened. Season to taste, then add the tarragon and

lemon juice, tasting again and adding a little more lemon juice if necessary. Remove from the heat and leave to stand for 2–3 minutes to allow the flavours to infuse, then strain the sauce and set aside, keeping warm.

4 Cook the radishes in plenty of boiling salted water for 5–6 minutes or until tender.

5 Cook the squid in boiling salted water for 2 minutes then drain well. Toss in a bowl with the olive oil, chives and some salt and pepper and set aside.

6 Meanwhile, season the salmon fillets and, working in batches if necessary, steam them, skin-side down, for 4–5 minutes or until cooked but still a little rare in the middle.

7 Divide the witlof choucroute among six plates, then top with a piece of salmon. Arrange the squid and radishes alongside the salmon and top with some watercress. Spoon the lemon sauce over the fish, then serve accompanied by a bowl of mixed salad leaves.

STEAMED FILLET OF BLUE-EYE TREVALLA WITH PRAWNS AND SAFFRON ARANCINI

SERVES 6

Blue-eye trevalla has a mild taste, and is available all year round. If possible, buy the trevalla and prawns on the day you are cooking them so they are at their freshest. These arancini are fun to make and add a distinctly Italian flavour.

2 vine-ripened tomatoes
¼ cup (60 ml) extra virgin olive oil
1 teaspoon coriander seeds, crushed
juice of 1 lemon
salt and pepper
2 tablespoons chopped flat-leaf parsley
3 teaspoons finely grated lemon zest
6 × 180 g blue-eye trevalla fillets
6 large raw king prawns, peeled,
   deveined and split lengthways
basil leaves, to garnish

SAFFRON ARANCINI
2 cups (500 ml) chicken stock
   (see page 222)
50 g butter
2 golden shallots, finely chopped
2 cloves garlic, finely chopped
large pinch of saffron threads
125 g risotto rice
1½ tablespoons white wine
50 g parmesan, grated
2½ tablespoons creme fraiche

1 tablespoon lemon juice
⅓ cup (50 g) plain flour
1 egg, lightly beaten
½ cup (50 g) dried breadcrumbs
vegetable oil, for shallow-frying
salt

1 To make the arancini, place the chicken stock in a saucepan and bring to the boil. In a separate heavy-based saucepan, melt the butter over medium heat, add the shallot and garlic and cook, stirring, for about 4 minutes or until the shallot is softened but not coloured. Add the saffron and rice and cook, stirring, for about 2 minutes or until the rice is heated through, then add the white wine. Bring to the boil, then add a ladleful of chicken stock. Simmer over medium heat, stirring, until the stock has been absorbed. Add another ladleful of hot stock and continue until the mixture is creamy and the rice is al dente. Remove the pan from the heat, stir in the parmesan, creme fraiche and lemon juice and season to taste. Pour the risotto out onto a large baking tray and leave to cool.

2 When the risotto is cold, divide it into small balls (you should get about 24 arancini). Place the flour, egg and breadcrumbs into separate bowls. Dust the balls in the flour, shaking off any excess, dip them into the egg, then cover in breadcrumbs.

3 Heat the vegetable oil in a heavy-based frying pan and shallow-fry the arancini in batches for 3–4 minutes or until deep golden, then remove with a slotted spoon and drain well on paper towel. Season well with salt, set aside and keep warm.

4 Meanwhile, use a small, sharp knife to cut a cross in the base of each tomato. Bring plenty of salted water to the boil in a large saucepan. Add the tomatoes and blanch for about 30 seconds, then remove with a slotted spoon and transfer to a bowl of iced water. Drain well, then peel the tomatoes and cut into quarters. Remove the seeds and dice the flesh.

5 Place the chopped tomato in a saucepan with the olive oil, crushed coriander seeds, lemon juice and a little salt and pepper. Warm over low heat; do not let it boil.

6 Combine the chopped parsley and lemon zest in a small bowl. Season the fish with salt and pepper then scatter a generous amount of the parsley and lemon zest onto each fillet and press it in.

7 Steam the fish for 5 minutes or until cooked through. Remove and keep warm, then add the prawns to the steamer and cook for 2 minutes or until cooked through. Remove the prawns and roughly chop.

8 To serve, place a piece of steamed fish on each plate, then arrange some arancini and chopped prawn around the fish. Dot around the warm tomato mixture and garnish with the basil.

MURRAY COD WITH BRAISED BORLOTTI BEANS IN MUSHROOM SAUCE

SERVES 6

This delicious seafood dish is great on a chilly winter's night. The different varieties of mushroom give the sauce a rich, deep flavour. King brown mushrooms, a type of oyster mushroom, have a very distinctive, strong flavour.

olive oil, for cooking
½ stalk celery, cut in half
½ onion, cut in half
½ carrot, cut in half
½ leek, well washed and cut in half
2 cloves garlic
250 g borlotti beans,
    from 500 g beans in pods
4 sprigs thyme
2 bay leaves
700 ml chicken stock (see page 222)
6 × 180 g Murray cod fillets

salt and pepper
25 g butter
6 small bunches English spinach,
    leaves removed and washed

MUSHROOM SAUCE
olive oil, for cooking
3 golden shallots, thinly sliced
2 cloves garlic, sliced
200 g button mushrooms, sliced
30 g dried porcini
100 ml Madeira

3 cups (750 ml) chicken stock
    (see page 222)
2 sprigs thyme
1 bay leaf
75 ml pouring cream
salt and pepper
2 king brown mushrooms, sliced
    lengthways into 3 and scored
    in a criss-cross motion
100 g chestnut mushrooms, trimmed
1½ tablespoons chopped
    flat-leaf parsley

1 Heat 1½ tablespoons oil in a large heavy-based saucepan over medium heat. Add the celery, onion, carrot, leek and garlic and cook for 2 minutes. Add the borlotti beans, thyme, bay leaves and chicken stock and bring to a simmer, then reduce the heat to low, cover and cook for 30 minutes or until the beans are tender. Remove from the heat and leave the beans to cool in the liquid, then drain the beans, discarding the flavourings, and set aside.

2 Meanwhile, to make the mushroom sauce, heat 1½ tablespoons oil in a heavy-based saucepan over medium heat, add the shallot and garlic and cook, stirring, for 3 minutes or until the shallot is softened. Add the mushrooms and porcini and cook, stirring, for 4–5 minutes or until the mushrooms are soft. Pour in the Madeira, bring to the boil, then cook for 3–4 minutes or until the liquid has reduced by half. Add the chicken stock, thyme and bay leaf, bring to the boil again and cook for about 10 minutes or until the liquid has reduced by half. Add the cream, reduce the heat to low and simmer for 5–6 minutes.

3 Meanwhile, heat a little more oil in a heavy-based frying pan over medium heat and add the king brown mushrooms. Cook for 3 minutes until golden, then add the chestnut mushrooms and cook for a further 2 minutes. Remove and add to the mushroom sauce, along with the drained borlotti beans and the chopped parsley, season to taste and place over low heat to keep the sauce warm while you cook the fish.

4 Wipe out the frying pan and heat ⅓ cup olive oil over medium–high heat. Add the fish, skin-side down, season and cook for 3 minutes until the skin is golden, then turn the fish over and cook for 2 minutes on the other side or until just cooked through. Transfer the fish to a plate to rest while you cook the spinach.

5 Melt the butter in a large saucepan over medium heat. Add the spinach, cover and cook, shaking the pan occasionally, for 2 minutes or until the spinach has wilted.

6 To serve, divide the wilted spinach among six plates, top each with a piece of fish and spoon some bean and mushroom mixture alongside.

OCEAN TROUT WITH CELERIAC AND HORSERADISH PUREE, SCHOOL PRAWNS AND RADISH

SERVES 6

School prawns have a shorter shelf life than king prawns or tiger prawns, so it is best to buy them on the day you intend to serve them. They are available all year round, but are at their peak between October and April. Celeriac makes a great puree that you could serve with almost any fish dish. If you can't find fresh horseradish, you can use the same amount of a good-quality horseradish sauce.

6 red radishes, trimmed and
    cut into quarters
1 litre vegetable oil, plus
    2 tablespoons extra
300 g school prawns
½ cup (75 g) plain flour, seasoned
    with salt and pepper
6 × 180 g ocean trout fillets, skin on
50 g butter
1½ tablespoons lemon juice

2½ tablespoons extra virgin olive oil
1 tablespoon chopped chives
handful watercress sprigs,
    leaves picked

CELERIAC AND HORSERADISH PUREE
1 head celeriac, peeled and cut
    into small pieces
50 g butter
½ cup (125 ml) vegetable stock
    (see page 222) or water
100 ml pouring cream
2½ tablespoons freshly grated
    horseradish, or to taste
salt and pepper

1 For the celeriac and horseradish puree, combine the celeriac, butter and stock in a small saucepan, cover and bring to a simmer. Cook over medium–low heat for 20 minutes or until the celeriac is tender and most of the liquid has been absorbed. Transfer to a blender or a food processor and process to a smooth puree. Return to the pan and stir in the cream and horseradish, then season to taste, cover and keep warm.

2 Cook the radishes in boiling salted water for 3 minutes or until tender. Drain well.

3 Heat 1 litre vegetable oil in a large heavy-based saucepan to 180°C or until a cube of bread turns golden in about 15 seconds. Dust the prawns in the flour, shaking off the excess, then deep-fry them for 1–2 minutes or until crisp. Drain well on paper towel and season with salt.

4 Heat the 2 tablespoons vegetable oil in a large non-stick frying pan over medium heat. Season the ocean trout with salt and pepper then add to the pan, skin-side down. Cook for 3 minutes then turn over and cook for another 2–3 minutes on the other side or until cooked but still a little rare in the middle. Add the butter to the pan and cook until it foams, then add the lemon juice, basting the fish with the juices two or three times.

5 Stir together the olive oil and chives in a small bowl.

6 Place a piece of fish in the centre of each plate and arrange the prawns, radish and watercress leaves around it. Spoon over a little of the chive oil and some celeriac and horseradish puree and serve.

SNAPPER AND SCALLOP PIE

SERVES 6–8

This pie is a great winter dish, perfect served with a salad, and tastes as impressive as it looks – but make sure you take the time to make homemade stock. The pastry is cooked separately to ensure that it is crisp all over and not soggy in the middle. A good trick to getting a nice glaze is to use a light hand when brushing on the eggwash.

---

8 pearl onions, peeled
2 cups (500 ml) fish stock
   (see page 223)
50 ml olive oil
1 leek, well washed, trimmed and diced
1 clove garlic, crushed
2 sprigs thyme
1 bay leaf
1 stalk celery, diced

50 ml dry vermouth
   (I like to use Noilly Prat)
30 g butter, diced
30 g plain flour
finely grated zest of 1 lemon
small handful dill, chopped
small handful flat-leaf parsley, chopped
400 g fresh scallops,
   cut in half widthways

600 g snapper fillet, diced
600 g puff pastry, thawed if frozen
2 egg yolks
salt

---

1 Cook the pearl onions in a saucepan of simmering water for 10–12 minutes or until tender, then drain and set aside.

2 Heat the fish stock over medium heat in a small saucepan.

3 Heat the olive oil over medium heat in a large heavy-based saucepan. Add the leek, garlic, thyme, bay leaf and celery and cook over low heat for about 5 minutes or until tender but not coloured. Add the vermouth and cook over medium heat for about 7 minutes or until the liquid has almost evaporated.

4 Remove and discard the bay leaf and thyme sprigs, then add the diced butter and flour and cook for 3–4 minutes, stirring continuously until incorporated and the flour is completely cooked.

5 Add the hot fish stock, a ladleful at a time, stirring continuously. Once all the stock has been added, cook for 2–3 minutes until a thick sauce consistency is achieved. Remove from the heat, cover and allow to cool.

6 When cooled to room temperature, add the lemon zest, dill, parsley, scallops, snapper and the cooked pearl onions and gently fold together, then transfer to a large baking dish. Cover with greaseproof paper, pressing it down onto the surface of the filling, and set aside.

7 Preheat the oven to 200°C and grease a large baking tray.

8 Roll out the pastry to a thickness of 5 mm and cut to generously fit the top of the baking dish. With the pastry on the benchtop, use the back of a spoon to press grooves into the surface of the pastry to resemble the scales of a fish. Transfer the pastry to the prepared baking tray. Mix the egg yolks with a splash of water and a pinch of salt and, using a pastry brush, lightly glaze the pastry.

9 Bake the pastry for 10 minutes, then place the baking dish with the filling in the oven. Cook the pastry and filling for 5 minutes, before reducing the oven temperature to 190°C. Cook for a further 10–15 minutes or until the pastry is puffed and golden brown and the filling is cooked through.

10 Carefully lift the cooked pastry and place over the baking dish to cover the filling before serving.

POULTRY AND GAME

POACHED TRUFFLED CHICKEN WITH SWEETCORN PANNA COTTA AND ALMOND PRALINE

SERVES 6

This dish is a knockout. You don't have to use truffles with the chicken, but they do add an earthy quality and make this dish all the more impressive. You can reuse the poaching liquid to make a delicious chicken soup.

50 g black truffle (optional)
6 chicken breast fillets, with skin on
1 stalk celery, chopped
1 leek, well washed, trimmed
   and chopped
1 carrot, chopped
2 cloves garlic, bruised
1 bay leaf
2 sprigs thyme
approximately 1.5 litres chicken
   stock (see page 222)
2 sweetcorn, husks and silks
   removed, kernels removed
   as described on page 33

1 tablespoon truffle oil
1½ tablespoons chopped chives
1½ tablespoons extra virgin olive oil
watercress sprigs, to serve

SWEETCORN PANNA COTTA
3 sweetcorn, husks and silks
   removed, kernels removed
   as described on page 33
25 g butter
1 cup (250 ml) chicken stock
   (see page 222)
200 ml milk
3 leaves gold-strength gelatine

ALMOND PRALINE
50 g caster sugar
50 g slivered almonds, toasted
1 teaspoon butter

VINAIGRETTE
1 teaspoon white wine vinegar
1 teaspoon champagne vinegar
½ teaspoon lemon juice
½ teaspoon Dijon mustard
salt and pepper
35 ml grapeseed oil

1 For the sweetcorn panna cotta, combine the corn kernels, butter and stock in a small saucepan over low–medium heat, bring to a simmer, then cover and cook for 35 minutes or until the kernels are soft. Transfer to a blender or food processor and process to a puree. Push the mixture through a sieve, pressing down to extract as much liquid as possible – you should have 300 ml of puree. Discard the solids. Combine the puree and the milk in a saucepan and bring just to a simmer then remove from the heat.

2 Soften the gelatine in cold water, then squeeze to extract as much water as possible and stir into the puree until dissolved. Cool to room temperature, then divide among six 100 ml moulds. Cover with plastic film and refrigerate for 2–3 hours or until set.

3 To make the praline, combine the sugar with 2 teaspoons water in a small saucepan. Bring slowly to the boil, then cook over medium heat for 5–6 minutes or until a dark caramel forms. Remove from the heat and add the almonds and butter, swirling the pan to combine well. Pour the mixture onto a piece of baking paper and leave to cool and harden, then chop into small pieces.

4 Finely slice the truffle, if using, then divide among the chicken breasts, pushing the slices under the skin.

5 Put the celery, leek, carrot, garlic, bay leaf and thyme in a large saucepan, then place the chicken neatly on top. Pour in enough stock to cover, then gradually bring the mixture barely to a simmer. Cover the pan and cook over very low heat for 20 minutes, then remove the pan from the heat and let the chicken cool in the liquid. Transfer the chicken to a chopping board then strain the liquid, discarding the solids, reserving the poaching liquid for another use.

6 Meanwhile, cook the corn kernels in boiling salted water for 10 minutes or until tender. Drain well and set aside to cool.

7 To make the vinaigrette, whisk together the vinegars, lemon juice and mustard, then season with salt and pepper. Whisking constantly, slowly pour in the grapeseed oil until combined.

8 To serve, briefly dip each panna cotta mould into hot water then carefully turn out onto serving plates. Slice each chicken breast widthways into three even pieces, then arrange on the plates and brush lightly with truffle oil.

9 Combine the corn kernels, chives and vinaigrette in a bowl, then spoon around the plates. Scatter over the praline, drizzle with olive oil and garnish with watercress.

POT-ROASTED JUMBO QUAIL WITH BABY ONIONS

SERVES 4

A great dinner party dish – maximum impact with minimum time and effort. If you are a bit nervous about trussing the quail, ask your butcher to do it for you. Swiss brown mushrooms hold their shape well while cooking, so are great to use here, but if you can't find any you could use chestnut mushrooms, which have a distinctive nutty taste, or button mushrooms instead.

---

4 jumbo quail
salt and pepper
vegetable oil, for cooking
50 g butter
12 pickling onions, peeled

250 g Swiss brown mushrooms,
    cut into wedges
250 g chestnut mushrooms
2 bay leaves
2 sprigs thyme

2½ tablespoons Madeira
1 cup (250 ml) chicken stock
    (see page 222)
300 g green beans, tops trimmed
olive oil, for drizzling

---

1 Preheat the oven to 170°C.

2 Truss the quail by passing a long piece of kitchen string underneath the back. Bring the ends of the string up around each leg and cross the ends over the top. Bring the string under the drumsticks and pull both ends to pull the legs together. Draw the ends of the string along either side of the quail and over the wing joints. Turn the quail onto its breast, cross the string over the back and tighten to pull the wings close to the body. Tie the string securely so the quail will keep its shape during cooking. Season well with salt and pepper.

3 Heat a little vegetable oil in a large flameproof casserole. Working in batches, brown the quail over medium heat for about 5 minutes or until golden, turning often. Remove the quail to a plate and drain the oil from the casserole, then wipe it clean with paper towel.

4 Return the casserole to the stove over medium heat and add the butter and a little more vegetable oil. Once the butter starts to foam, add the peeled onions, then season and cook for about 2 minutes or until the onions have coloured. Add the mushrooms, bay leaves and thyme and cook for 2 minutes, then turn the heat up to high and add the Madeira. Bring to the boil and cook for 1 minute, then add the chicken stock and cook for 2 minutes.

5 Return the quail to the casserole and cover with a tight-fitting lid or some foil. Place in the oven for approximately 15 minutes or until cooked (to test, pierce the thickest part of the bird with a skewer; the juices should run clear).

6 Remove the casserole from the oven, take off the lid and leave to rest for 5 minutes.

7 Meanwhile, blanch the green beans in plenty of boiling salted water for 2–3 minutes, then drain well and transfer to a large serving bowl. Drizzle with olive oil.

8 Serve the quail in a large serving dish at the table, with the bowl of green beans alongside.

ROAST DUCK BREAST WITH PICKLED RED CABBAGE AND FIGS

SERVES 4

For a special occasion, this dish is hard to beat. The combination of flavours works so well – the sweetish cabbage and the spicy jus really enhance the duck. Your guests will be amazed.

---

4 x 180–200 g duck breasts, skin scored
salt and pepper
olive oil, for cooking
2 figs, cut into wedges
1 small handful frisee
   (curly endive) leaves
1 small handful baby parsley or
   flat-leaf parsley leaves

PICKLED RED CABBAGE
1 small red cabbage, very finely sliced
100 g sea salt
200 ml red wine vinegar
50 ml balsamic vinegar

100 ml red wine
300 g caster sugar
1 star anise, crushed
1 teaspoon coriander seeds, crushed
1 teaspoon juniper berries, crushed
1 teaspoon black peppercorns, crushed
6 cloves, crushed
½ cinnamon stick, crushed
1 teaspoon dried chilli flakes

SPICED DUCK JUS
olive oil, for cooking
500 g duck wings
6 golden shallots, sliced

2 cloves garlic, sliced
2 sprigs thyme
1 bay leaf
1 x 4 cm piece ginger, sliced
1 cinnamon stick
3 star anise
2 juniper berries
1 teaspoon mustard seeds
100 ml port
2 cups (500 ml) chicken stock
   (see page 222)
2 cups (500 ml) veal jus
   (see page 224)
salt and pepper

---

1 To make the pickled cabbage, mix the cabbage with the sea salt in a bowl, cover and set aside for 4 hours, then rinse under cold water and drain well. Set aside in a bowl.

2 Combine the vinegars, red wine, sugar and 50 ml water in a saucepan and heat over high heat for 10 minutes, stirring occasionally, until syrupy. Add the spices and leave to infuse for 5 minutes over low–medium heat, then strain the liquid through a fine-meshed sieve into the bowl with the cabbage. Mix well and leave in the fridge overnight.

3 To make the jus, heat a little oil over medium heat in a large heavy-based saucepan and cook the duck wings for about 15 minutes or until golden, stirring occasionally. Add the shallot, garlic, herbs and spices and cook for 3–4 minutes until fragrant. Increase the heat to high and add the port, stirring and scraping with a wooden spoon to get all the meaty bits off the bottom of the pan, then cook for 2–3 minutes before adding the stock and veal jus. Cook for 40 minutes over medium heat, then strain the mixture through a fine-meshed sieve into a clean pan, discarding the solids.

4 Place the pan over a medium–high heat and cook for about 10 minutes or until reduced to a sauce consistency. Season to taste, set aside and keep warm.

5 Preheat the oven to 200°C.

6 Season the duck breasts with salt and pepper. Heat the oil in an ovenproof frying pan over medium heat and add the duck breasts, skin-side down. Cook for 4–5 minutes, then turn and cook the other side for 1–2 minutes. Turn the duck breasts skin-side down again, then transfer the pan to the oven and cook for 6 minutes. Remove the duck breasts from the pan and set aside in a warm place to rest for 10 minutes, before slicing each breast evenly.

7 Meanwhile, heat the pickled cabbage in a saucepan over low heat to warm through.

8 Spoon some cabbage onto each plate, and top with a sliced duck breast. Place a few fig wedges alongside and garnish with frisee and parsley leaves. Drizzle over the spiced duck jus and serve.

SAUTEED CHICKEN WITH CHORIZO AND CHICKPEAS

SERVES 4

The spices and harissa give this dish a distinctly Middle-Eastern flavour. If you are feeling brave, you could use another tablespoon of harissa for added bite. You can halve the quantities of the candied lemon zest here, or make a big batch and store the leftovers in an airtight container at room temperature for several days, or in the fridge for several weeks. It can be chopped up and added to salads, biscuits or cake mixes, or you could add some chopped zest and syrup to vodka for a delicious cocktail.

½ cup (100 g) dried chickpeas, soaked
    overnight then drained
1 × 1.6 kg corn-fed free-range chicken,
    cut into 8 pieces
salt and pepper
2 tablespoons vegetable oil
25 g butter
1 small brown onion, finely chopped
3 cloves garlic, finely chopped

1 chorizo sausage (about 100 g),
    thinly sliced
1 teaspoon ground cumin
1 teaspoon ground coriander
1 tablespoon harissa
300 ml chicken jus (see page 224)
1 head cavolo nero
    (Tuscan kale), trimmed
coriander leaves, to garnish

CANDIED LEMON ZEST
zest of 4 lemons, removed in strips
    with a vegetable peeler
1 cup (220 g) caster sugar
1 vanilla bean, split and seeds scraped
1 star anise
2 cloves garlic, bruised

1 To make the candied lemon zest, place the lemon zest into a saucepan of salted water and bring to the boil, then remove from the heat and leave to cool in the water. Meanwhile, combine the caster sugar and 1 cup (250 ml) water in a saucepan and bring to the boil over low heat, stirring to dissolve the sugar. Add the vanilla pod and seeds, star anise and garlic to the syrup, along with the cooled lemon zest, and bring to the boil again. Cover the surface with a piece of baking paper, reduce the heat to very low and cook for 1 hour, then turn off the heat and leave in the pan to cool. Once cooled, reserve a couple of pieces of zest and transfer the remainder to an airtight container for another use.

2 Place the chickpeas in a small saucepan of cold water, bring to a simmer then cook over low–medium heat for 45 minutes or until tender. Drain well.

3 Season the chicken pieces well with salt and pepper. Heat the vegetable oil over medium heat in a large heavy-based casserole, add the chicken and cook, turning occasionally, for 6–7 minutes or until browned all over. Transfer the chicken pieces to a plate and drain off any excess oil left in the casserole. Return it to the heat, melt the butter then throw in the onion, garlic and chorizo and cook, stirring, for 2–3 minutes or until the onion has softened slightly. Add the cumin, coriander and harissa and cook, stirring, for another 2 minutes, before adding back the browned chicken pieces. Pour in the chicken jus, stirring to dislodge any stuck-on bits from the base of the pan, then bring to the boil over high heat. Add the chickpeas, reduce the heat to medium, cover and simmer for about 10 minutes or until the chicken is cooked through.

4 Meanwhile, cook the cavolo nero in plenty of boiling salted water for 5–6 minutes until tender, then drain well.

5 Roughly chop the reserved candied lemon zest and scatter over the chicken with some coriander leaves. Serve the casserole at the table for people to help themselves, with the cavolo nero alongside.

RED-BRAISED SPATCHCOCK WITH BOK CHOY AND CONSOMME

SERVES 6

The best way to approach this recipe is to start preparing the various components ahead of time. None of them is particularly difficult – they just take a little time. So, you could easily prepare the chicken consomme (steps 1–8) a day or two in advance, keep it in the fridge and then gently reheat it when you use it. You could also make the master stock the day before, and leave the spatchcock to marinate in it overnight (steps 9–10). Then all you have to do on the day is cook the spatchcock (step 11) and prepare the vegetables (steps 12–14), and voila – you have a restaurant-quality dinner! The sweetly spiced master stock is a key ingredient of this dish. I have had my master stock in the freezer for 8 years now and it develops more and more flavour every time I use it. After you've used it to cook the spatchcock, bring it to the boil, skim any scum off the top, then let it cool to room temperature and freeze it for next time.

3 spatchcock, cut in half,
   backbone removed
9 shiitake mushrooms, thickly sliced
3 heads baby bok choy, leaves separated
½ long cucumber, cut into batons
1 spring onion, very finely sliced
   on the diagonal
1 small handful baby coriander
   or regular coriander, to garnish

CHICKEN CONSOMME
3 kg chicken bones
1 pig's trotter
1 carrot, coarsely chopped
1 onion, coarsely chopped
2 stalks celery, coarsely chopped
1 leek, trimmed and coarsely chopped
2 cloves garlic, peeled
grapeseed or peanut oil, for cooking
1½ tablespoons tomato paste
1 sprig thyme
5 bay leaves
1 cup (250 ml) white wine
3 litres chicken stock (see page 222)
150 g chicken breast fillet, chopped
6 egg whites

MASTER STOCK
1 cup (250 ml) rice wine vinegar
150 g palm sugar, chopped
1 × 4 cm piece ginger, sliced
2 star anise
2 cinnamon sticks
1 cup (250 ml) light soy sauce
2½ tablespoons sherry vinegar
3 × 1 cm wide strips orange zest

PICKLED DAIKON
1 × 500 g piece daikon, cut into batons
2½ tablespoons rice wine vinegar
1½ tablespoons caster sugar
1½ tablespoons soy sauce

1 Firstly, to make the consomme, preheat the oven to 180°C. Place the chicken bones and the trotter in a roasting tin, and the chopped vegetables and garlic in a separate roasting tin, splash some oil in both tins and place in the oven.

2 After 30 minutes, remove the tin with the vegetables and stir through the tomato paste, then return the tin to the oven and continue roasting both the vegetables and the chicken for 15 minutes or until deep golden.

3 Remove both tins from the oven and transfer the contents to a large heavy-based saucepan or a stockpot. Add the thyme, bay leaves and wine, bring to a simmer, then cook for 10 minutes over medium heat or until the wine has reduced by half.

4 Add the chicken stock and bring the mixture to a simmer, skimming off any scum that rises to the surface, then reduce the heat to low and cook for 4–6 hours, skimming occasionally and making sure it does not boil (the longer you cook it for, the greater the depth of flavour will be).

5 Remove the pan from the heat and strain the contents through a muslin-lined sieve, discarding the solids, then set the stock aside to cool to room temperature.

6 Place the chopped chicken breast and the egg whites into a food processor and process to a fine paste. **>**

7 Return the cooled stock to the saucepan and slowly whisk in the chicken mixture, then place over high heat, stirring occasionally. As the stock heats, the chicken mixture will start to coagulate, rising to the top to form a layer, or a 'raft', on the surface of the stock. When this happens, turn the heat down to very low to ensure the stock doesn't boil, as boiling will ruin the clarification. Simmer very gently for 10 minutes, then carefully make a hole in the centre of the raft to enable the stock to 'breathe' – make sure the hole is big enough to fit a ladle through, ready for when the time comes to remove the clarified stock. Simmer for another 30–40 minutes; during this time, the stock should become crystal clear.

8 Carefully ladle the clarified stock out of the saucepan (taking care not to disturb the raft as this will cloud the consomme) into a muslin-lined sieve placed over a large clean saucepan, then set aside.

9 To make the master stock, combine all the ingredients with 1 litre water in a large heavy-based saucepan or stockpot and bring to the boil, then simmer for 15 minutes. Strain the contents, discarding the solids, and leave the stock to cool to room temperature.

10 Place the spatchcock halves in a large bowl or container and pour over enough cooled master stock to cover. Cover and refrigerate for 6 hours.

11 Remove the spatchcock from the fridge and transfer to a large heavy-based pan along with the stock it was soaking in. Bring to the boil and simmer for 15 minutes, then remove the spatchcock from the pan with a slotted spoon and cover to keep warm.

12 Add the shiitake mushrooms to the stock, cover and remove the pan from the heat. Drain just before serving.

13 Meanwhile, to make the pickled daikon, place the daikon in a saucepan with the other ingredients and 100 ml water. Bring to a simmer over medium–high heat and cook for 2–3 minutes, then remove the pan from the heat and cover to keep warm.

14 Bring a large saucepan of salted water to the boil, add the bok choy and cook for 1 minute or just until wilted. Remove with a slotted spoon and drain well. Add the cucumber to the boiling water and cook for 30 seconds or until just softened, then drain well.

15 Reheat the consomme over low–medium heat and simmer until warmed through.

16 To serve, arrange the wilted bok choy in the centre of six shallow serving bowls. Place a spatchcock half on top, then arrange the cucumber, pickled daikon and drained shiitake mushrooms over, sprinkling around the spring onion and scattering over some coriander. Ladle over the hot consomme to finish.

ASIAN-INSPIRED DINNER

SERVES 6

There is no need to order in or dine out for quality Asian food when you can pull a dinner like this out of your repertoire. This is the perfect menu for dinner on a warm summer's evening. Just make sure that you leave yourself plenty of time to prepare the spatchcock – you may want to start it the day before. The combination of flavours in this menu is quite stunning. The soup and tuna each have quite a delicate taste, whereas the spatchcock has a much richer flavour. The decadent cheesecake dessert adds a lovely touch of whimsy.

FRICASSEE OF CHICKEN WITH PEAS, BABY ONIONS AND COS LETTUCE

SERVES 4–6

This is a wonderful dinner party dish (pictured overleaf). The vermouth gives it a great flavour and the creamy sauce is beautifully rich without being overwhelming. If you prefer, ask your butcher to cut the chicken into pieces for you.

---

1 × 1.5 kg chicken
salt and pepper
2½ tablespoons vegetable oil
75 g butter, plus extra to finish
12 golden shallots, finely sliced
2 cloves garlic, crushed
250 g button mushrooms, sliced
150 ml dry vermouth
   (I like to use Noilly Prat)
4 sprigs thyme

1 bay leaf
1.25 litres chicken stock
   (see page 222)
1½ cups (375 ml) pouring cream
300 g baby onions, peeled,
   leaving root end intact
3 large desiree potatoes,
   cut into 1 cm pieces
300 g fresh peas (from about
   600 g peas in pods)

1 cos lettuce, large outer leaves
   removed and discarded
shaved black truffle, optional, to serve
small handful tarragon leaves

---

1 Using a large sharp knife, remove the marylands from the chicken by cutting through the upper thigh joint. Separate the marylands into legs and thighs by cutting through the lower thigh joint. Cut down either side of the backbone and remove it, reserving it for making stock. Cut down the breast bone to separate the breasts then cut each breast into two pieces, leaving the wings attached to the upper breast. Season the chicken pieces well with salt and pepper.

2 Heat the oil in a large heavy-based pan over medium heat and, working in batches if necessary, cook the chicken pieces for 5 minutes, turning occasionally, or until light golden all over. Remove the chicken pieces with a slotted spoon, drain on paper towel and set aside.

3 Add the butter to the pan and melt over low–medium heat, then add the shallot and garlic and cook, stirring often, for 7–8 minutes or until the shallot has softened. Add the mushrooms and cook for 8–9 minutes or until the mushrooms are tender and most of the moisture has evaporated. Add the vermouth, increase the heat to high and simmer for 3–4 minutes or until reduced to a glaze. Add the herbs and chicken stock, bring to the boil and cook for 4–5 minutes or until the liquid has reduced by half. Add the cream, bring to the boil again and cook for 3–4 minutes or until the liquid has reduced by half.

4 Add the chicken pieces to the sauce, check for seasoning, then bring the mixture to a simmer and cook over low–medium heat for 20 minutes or until the chicken is cooked through.

5 Meanwhile, cook the pearl onions in plenty of boiling salted water for 7–8 minutes or until tender, then drain.

6 Cook the potatoes in plenty of boiling salted water for 6–7 minutes or until tender, then drain.

7 Blanch the peas in plenty of boiling salted water for 3 minutes, then drain.

8 Stir the cos lettuce through the chicken and sauce and cook for 1–2 minutes over low–medium heat until just wilted. Add the onions and peas and stir through, then transfer to a large serving dish and scatter over a few shavings of black truffle, if using.

9 Transfer the potato to a small bowl, season well with salt and pepper, sprinkle with tarragon leaves and finish with a knob of butter. Serve both dishes at the table for guests to help themselves.

ROAST CHICKEN WITH CARROTS AND CELERIAC PUREE

SERVES 4

Everyone loves roast chicken, and this recipe is foolproof. Instead of the usual roast potatoes and pumpkin, I like to serve the chicken with this distinctive celeriac puree. This is a great way to cook carrots, too – the caramelised honey and cumin are a perfect match.

olive oil, for pan-frying
1 × 1.6 kg chicken
salt and pepper
chervil sprigs, to garnish

CELERIAC PUREE
1 tablespoon olive oil
30 g butter, diced
1 leek, white part only,
    well washed and diced
2 cloves garlic, crushed
1 bay leaf
1 sprig thyme
1 large head celeriac,
    peeled and finely diced
2 cups (500 ml) chicken stock
    (see page 222) or to cover
salt and pepper

ROAST CARROTS
500 g baby (Dutch) carrots,
    washed and trimmed
1 tablespoon cumin seeds, toasted
½ cup (180 g) honey
2 tablespoons olive oil
salt and pepper

1 Preheat the oven to 180°C.

2 Heat a little oil in a large frying pan over medium heat. Season the chicken with salt and pepper, then place in the pan, breast-side down, and reduce the heat to low–medium. Cook for 8–10 minutes, turning the chicken to caramelise all over, or until the skin is golden brown.

3 Place the chicken in a roasting tin and cook in the oven for 1 hour or until the juices run clear when the meat is pierced with a skewer. Remove and rest for 15 minutes.

4 Meanwhile, to prepare the roast carrots, line a baking tray with non-stick baking paper. Toss all the ingredients together in a bowl, then transfer to the prepared tray and roast for 10–15 minutes or until golden.

5 For the celeriac puree, heat the oil and butter in a saucepan over medium heat. Add the leek, garlic, bay leaf and thyme and cook for 4–5 minutes or until soft but not coloured. Add the celeriac and stock and season with salt and pepper. Bring to a simmer, then cook for 15–20 minutes or until soft. Remove the thyme and bay leaf, then puree the mixture with a hand-held blender until smooth. Cover and keep warm.

6 Serve the chicken and carrots on a large board, garnish with chervil and serve the celeriac puree alongside.

PHEASANT WITH SAVOY CABBAGE AND BREAD SAUCE

SERVES 6

Quickly sealed, roasted with plenty of butter and then rested, pheasant meat is sweet and succulent – a real treat for your guests. Served simply with cabbage and an old-fashioned bread sauce, this is the perfect dish for a late autumn dinner party. Just remember to order the pheasants from your butcher in advance.

olive oil, for cooking
2 pheasants
salt and pepper
100 g butter
½ Savoy cabbage, shredded
    into 1 cm strips

1 tablespoon duck fat or olive oil
1 carrot, cut into small batons
150 g pancetta, cut into lardons

BREAD SAUCE
1 cup (250 ml) milk
¼ onion
1 clove
1 bay leaf
1 pinch nutmeg
50 g fresh breadcrumbs
salt and pepper

1 Preheat the oven to 180°C.

2 Heat a little oil over medium heat in a large ovenproof frying pan. Season the pheasants with salt and pepper, then cook, turning often, for 3–4 minutes or until golden all over. Turn the birds breast-side up, add the butter to the pan and transfer to the oven. Roast for 15 minutes, basting occasionally with the melted butter, then remove from the oven and set aside to rest for 10 minutes.

3 To make the bread sauce, place the milk, onion, clove and bay leaf in a saucepan and warm over medium heat. Bring to a simmer, then remove from the heat and set aside to infuse for 10–15 minutes.

4 Blanch the cabbage in plenty of boiling salted water for 2 minutes, then drain and set aside.

5 Heat the duck fat or oil in a frying pan over medium heat then add the carrot and pancetta, reduce the heat to low and cook for 2–3 minutes or until tender. Stir through the blanched cabbage, then season and keep warm until ready to serve.

6 Return the sauce to the heat and bring to the boil, then add the nutmeg and breadcrumbs and cook over low–medium heat for 4–5 minutes, stirring occasionally. Season with salt and pepper.

7 Remove the breast and legs from the pheasants. To serve, place some cabbage on each plate with a leg and breast on top, then spoon some bread sauce to one side.

BRAISED CHICKEN WITH MUSHROOMS AND TAGLIATELLE

SERVES 4–6

For a dish like this, it's generally less expensive to buy a whole chicken and cut it up yourself rather than buying pre-cut pieces. To prepare it as required here, cut it on the bone into eight pieces: two pieces each of chicken breast, thigh, leg and boneless cutlet. I use button mushrooms in the sauce, but when you are deciding which mushrooms to serve on top you can experiment a little. I like to use girolle mushrooms (sometimes called chanterelles), which have a particularly rich flavour, or trumpet mushrooms, which have a very sweet smell. If you can't find these, you can just as easily use the more common Swiss browns.

---

50 g butter
300 g mushrooms, sliced
2 tablespoons finely chopped
    flat-leaf parsley

PASTA DOUGH
500 g 'OO' pasta flour
pinch of salt
2½ tablespoons olive oil
2 eggs
8 egg yolks

BRAISED CHICKEN
olive oil, for pan-frying
salt and pepper
1 × 1.4 kg chicken, cut into 8 pieces
50 g butter
2 cloves garlic, sliced
3 sprigs thyme
200 g golden shallots, sliced
200 g button mushrooms, sliced
½ cup (125 ml) sherry
1.5 litres chicken stock (see page 222)
⅓ cup (80 ml) pouring cream

---

1 For the pasta dough, combine the flour, salt and olive oil in a food processor and process until the mixture resembles fine breadcrumbs. With the motor running, add the eggs and egg yolks and combine well. Tip the dough onto a clean benchtop and knead briefly until smooth and elastic, then wrap in plastic film and refrigerate for 1 hour.

2 Meanwhile, for the braised chicken, preheat the oven to 150°C. Heat a little olive oil in a frying pan. Lightly season the chicken pieces, then add them to the pan and seal on both sides. Remove and set aside.

3 Melt the butter in a flameproof casserole over medium heat, add the garlic, thyme and shallot and cook, stirring, for 6–7 minutes or until softened. Add the mushrooms and cook for 5 minutes or until softened. Pour in the sherry and bring to a simmer, then cook for 6–7 minutes or until the sherry has reduced by two-thirds. Add the stock and the chicken pieces and bring to the boil, then cover and transfer to the oven to cook for 40 minutes or until the chicken is cooked through.

4 Divide the pasta dough into three equal pieces and flatten with your hands. Working with one piece at a time (and keeping the others covered with a damp tea towel to prevent them drying out), roll through a pasta machine, starting at the highest setting then working through to the lowest. Very lightly flour the pasta sheet and gently fold it, then store under the damp tea towel while you roll the remaining sheets. Cut the pasta sheets into strips about 5 mm wide.

5 Remove the chicken pieces from the casserole with a slotted spoon and set aside. Discard the thyme sprigs then transfer the remaining contents of the casserole to a blender or food processor and process until smooth. Strain through a sieve into a large saucepan, pressing down on the solids to extract as much liquid as possible, then discard the solids. Bring the liquid to a simmer and cook over medium heat for 15–20 minutes or until reduced and thickened slightly. Stir in the cream and season to taste, then return the chicken to the sauce and reheat.

6 Melt the butter in a large frying pan over medium heat, add the mushrooms and cook, stirring, for 5 minutes. Meanwhile, bring a large saucepan of salted water to the boil, add the tagliatelle and cook for 2–3 minutes or until al dente. Drain well, then divide among pasta bowls.

7 Spoon over the braised chicken and sauce and place the mushrooms on top. Scatter with parsley and serve.

TANDOORI SPATCHCOCK

SERVES 6

For best results, start this dish the day before so that the spatchcock can marinate overnight. The combination of spices in the marinade gives the spatchcock a really fantastic flavour. Crisp-fried onions are available from Asian grocers, and you might also like to serve this dish with steamed rice or couscous.

6 spatchcock
1 teaspoon salt
2½ tablespoons lemon juice
seeds from 1 tablespoon
    cardamom pods
1 cinnamon stick
1 teaspoon cumin seeds

1 teaspoon cloves
1 teaspoon black peppercorns
1 teaspoon grated nutmeg
1 small golden shallot, chopped
2 cloves garlic
1 × 2.5 cm piece ginger
1 fresh red chilli

3 tablespoons tomato paste
1 cup (250 g) Greek-style yoghurt
vegetable oil, for cooking
crisp-fried onions and finely sliced
    fresh chilli, to serve

1 Using a sharp knife, cut the legs of the spatchcock through the upper thigh, then remove them by cutting through the lower thigh joint. Cut through either side of the backbone, then discard the backbone or reserve for making stock. Place the breasts skin-side down, then cut in half through the breast bone. Cut each breast in half widthways. Season all the pieces with salt and rub them all over with lemon juice. Place in a large non-reactive bowl, cover and refrigerate for 20 minutes.

2 To prepare the spice mixture, place the cardamom seeds, cinnamon, cumin seeds, cloves, peppercorns and nutmeg in a mortar or electric spice grinder. Grind the mixture to a fine powder then store in an airtight jar until required.

3 Place the shallot, garlic, ginger, chilli, tomato paste, yoghurt and 2 teaspoons of the spice mixture into a blender and blend to a smooth paste. Coat the spatchcock pieces in the paste and leave to marinate, covered, for 24 hours in the refrigerator.

4 Preheat the oven to 180°C and drizzle a little oil into a baking dish.

5 Preheat the barbecue to its hottest setting or place a chargrill pan over high heat. Remove the meat from the marinade, shaking off any excess, then grill for 2–3 minutes each side before transferring to the baking dish. Cook in the oven for about 18 minutes or until cooked through.

6 Serve the spatchcock with plenty of crisp-fried onions and fresh chilli scattered over.

MEAT

ROAST VEAL LOIN WITH SHALLOT TARTE TATIN AND HORSERADISH CREME FRAICHE

SERVES 6

It is a good idea to make a big batch of bordelaise sauce (see page 225) when you have the time and the inclination, and then keep containers of it in the freezer, so that you have it on hand for recipes like this. It is easy to make in large quantities, and adds real refinement to many meat dishes. You'll need six individual 9 cm tarte tatin moulds for this recipe. The finished product is fantastic – the sweet flavour of the tartes tatins and the piquant horseradish cream set off the veal beautifully.

---

2 tablespoons vegetable oil
1.2 kg trimmed veal loin
1 large bunch silverbeet
   (Swiss chard), leaves removed,
   washed and coarsely chopped
20 g butter
salt and pepper
150 ml bordelaise sauce
   (see page 225), warmed

HORSERADISH CREME FRAICHE
1 tablespoon good-quality
   horseradish cream, or to taste
100 g creme fraiche
2 teaspoons finely chopped chives
salt and pepper

SHALLOT TARTE TATIN
30–36 golden shallots,
   peeled, leaving root
   end intact
1 cup (220 g) caster sugar
20 g butter
200 ml sherry vinegar
2 sheets puff pastry (thawed if frozen)

---

1 For the horseradish creme fraiche, place all the ingredients in a small bowl and stir to combine, adding a little extra horseradish cream if desired. Taste and check the seasoning, then cover and refrigerate until required.

2 To make the shallot tarte tatin, bring a large saucepan of salted water to the boil, add the shallots and cook for 3 minutes or just until softened. Drain the shallots and cool them to room temperature.

3 Dissolve the sugar in a large heavy-based frying pan over medium heat, then cook for about 3 minutes or until a caramel forms. Add the butter and swirl to combine (take care as the mixture will spit), then add the shallots and vinegar and toss to combine well. Simmer for 3–4 minutes or until the caramel coats the shallots. Remove the shallots from the pan, reserving the caramel, and set aside to cool.

4 Preheat the oven to 180°C.

5 Neatly divide the cooled shallots among six 9 cm tarte tatin moulds and spoon over a little of the reserved caramel. Cut six rounds from the pastry using a 9 cm cutter. Place one round over each tart, pushing the sides in around the shallots to form a cup shape over the top. Bake for 20 minutes or until the pastry is golden brown.

6 Meanwhile, heat the vegetable oil in a large ovenproof frying pan over high heat and seal all sides of the veal loin.

7 Place the frying pan in the oven for 20 minutes or until the veal is cooked but still a little pink in the middle. Remove and rest the meat for 10 minutes before cutting into thick slices.

8 Blanch the silverbeet in a large saucepan of boiling salted water for 2–3 minutes, then remove and drain on paper towel. Toss in a pan with the butter over medium heat for a minute or two, then drain off any excess liquid and season to taste.

9 To serve, place a mound of silverbeet on each plate and arrange a couple of slices of veal on top. Place a tarte tatin on each plate and top with a spoonful of horseradish creme fraiche. Spoon some warmed bordelaise sauce over the veal and serve.

ROAST PORK CUTLETS WITH HIBISCUS-POACHED PEARS, WITLOF AND BEANS

SERVES 6

This very elegant dish looks wildly impressive on the plate and is not all that difficult to prepare – just leave yourself plenty of time. The combination of flavours works really well, and the poached pears add a lovely touch of sweetness. Paradise pears are very small, sweet pears available between February and April. If you can't get hold of dried hibiscus flowers, you can add grenadine to the poaching liquid instead (about 50 ml will give the pears the same pink hue).

2 tablespoons vegetable oil
6 pork cutlets, skin removed
400 g green beans, tops trimmed
220 ml mustard sauce
   (see page 225), warmed
6 sprigs tarragon, leaves picked

HIBISCUS-POACHED PEARS
2 tablespoons dried hibiscus flowers
150 g caster sugar
1 star anise
2 x 1 cm wide strips lemon zest
2 tablespoons red wine vinegar
12 paradise pears, peeled

GLAZED WITLOF
1 tablespoon vegetable oil
6 witlof (chicory), cut in half lengthways
1½ tablespoons caster sugar
2½ tablespoons chardonnay vinegar
30 g butter

1 For the poached pears, tie the hibiscus flowers in a muslin bag and place in a small saucepan with the sugar, star anise, lemon zest, vinegar and 2 cups (500 ml) water. Bring to the boil, then remove from the heat and set aside for 20 minutes to allow the flavours to infuse. Return to the heat and bring to a simmer, add the pears and cook over low heat for 12 minutes or until tender. Leave the pears to cool in the liquid.

2 For the glazed witlof, heat the oil in a large frying pan over medium heat. Add the witlof, cut-side down, and cook for 2–3 minutes or until it starts to caramelise, then remove to a plate. Increase the heat to medium–high, add the sugar, vinegar and butter and cook for 3 minutes or until the mixture turns a caramel colour. Return the witlof to the pan, cut-side up, and cook for 2 minutes or until the liquid has reduced and thickened slightly. Keep warm until ready to serve.

3 Meanwhile, working in batches, heat the vegetable oil in a large frying pan over medium heat, add the cutlets and cook for 5–6 minutes on each side or until just cooked through.

4 Cook the beans in plenty of boiling salted water for 3–4 minutes or until tender. Drain well and slice lengthways, if desired.

5 To serve, divide the green beans, pears and witlof among six plates. Carve each cutlet into three thick slices and place on top of the beans, then spoon over the mustard sauce and scatter with tarragon leaves.

ROAST LOIN OF LAMB WITH EGGPLANT CAVIAR, RED CAPSICUM AND GREEN OLIVE SAUCE

SERVES 6

I love to cook with lamb loin, one of the sweetest and most tender cuts of lamb. The combination of eggplant, capsicum and zucchini, with its echoes of ratatouille, goes beautifully with the lamb. The lavender petals add a hint of sweetness to the jus.

2 large red capsicum (peppers)
3 tablespoons extra virgin olive oil
1 clove garlic, bruised
1 teaspoon chopped thyme
salt and pepper
⅓ cup (80 ml) vegetable oil
6 × 150 g lamb loins, trimmed of
    excess fat
65 g butter
2 zucchini (courgette), cut widthways at
    an angle into slices about 1 cm thick

1 cup (250 ml) lamb jus (see page 225)
2 tablespoons chopped pitted
    green olives
2 teaspoons fresh lavender petals

EGGPLANT CAVIAR

2 teaspoons finely chopped thyme
½ teaspoon ground cumin
2 cloves garlic, crushed
¼ cup (60 ml) extra virgin olive oil
salt and pepper
2 medium-sized eggplant (aubergine),
    cut in half lengthways,
    flesh scored
1 golden shallot, finely chopped
1 tablespoon lemon juice

1 To make the eggplant caviar, preheat the oven to 170°C.

2 Combine the thyme, cumin, half the garlic and half the olive oil in a small bowl, season well and stir to combine. Spread this mixture evenly over the scored surface of the eggplant halves, then place the halves together and wrap tightly in foil. Roast for 20 minutes, or until the flesh of the eggplant is soft. When cool enough to handle, use a spoon to scoop out the flesh into a colander, and leave to stand for 30 minutes for any excess liquid to drain out.

3 Heat the remaining olive oil in a saucepan over low–medium heat, add the shallot and the remaining garlic and cook, stirring, for 3 minutes or until the shallot has softened. Add the drained eggplant flesh then cook, stirring often, for 6–7 minutes or until any excess liquid has evaporated and the mixture forms a thick puree. Add the lemon juice, season to taste and set aside.

4 Cook the capsicum over a gas flame, turning often, for 7–8 minutes or until charred all over (or roast in the oven at the highest temperature for 5–6 minutes). Transfer to a bowl, cover with plastic film and allow to cool, then peel off the blackened skin. Cut the capsicum open and remove the seeds and membrane, then slice in half lengthways. Place on a board, opening the capsicums up to flatten them, slice into 1 cm wide strips and transfer to a bowl. Drizzle over the olive oil, toss in the bruised garlic and thyme and season with salt and pepper. Set aside to marinate for 20 minutes, then drain.

5 Preheat the oven to 180°C.

6 Heat half the vegetable oil in a large ovenproof frying pan over medium–high heat then add the lamb loins and cook on each side for 1–2 minutes or until browned. Add the butter and, when melted, baste the lamb loins before transferring the pan to the oven. Roast for 4–6 minutes or until the lamb is cooked through but still a little pink in the middle.

7 Remove the pan from the oven, cover loosely with foil and set aside to rest for 5–10 minutes.

8 Heat the remaining oil in a frying pan over medium–high heat, add the zucchini then cook, turning often, for 5–6 minutes or until golden brown all over.

9 Combine the lamb jus, olives and lavender petals in a small saucepan and bring just to a simmer. Gently reheat the eggplant caviar until warmed through.

10 To serve, slice each lamb loin into three even pieces and arrange on plates. Spoon on dollops of eggplant caviar, and place some zucchini and capsicum alongside. Spoon over the sauce and serve immediately.

BEEF WELLINGTON WITH ASPARAGUS AND MASH

SERVES 4

A big hit at dinner parties in the 70s, Beef Wellington (pictured overleaf) is currently enjoying a bit of a revival. I prefer it with this mushroom stuffing, rather than the traditional pate, as it's much lighter. The crepes inserted between the meat and the pastry prevent the pastry from getting soggy. The amount given here makes three crepes, so you have a spare if one doesn't work. To create this impressive lattice pattern in the pastry you will need a lattice dough cutter, available from specialty kitchen supply stores.

1 x 500 g centre-cut beef fillet
   (10–12 cm long)
salt and pepper
olive oil, for cooking
2 egg yolks
2 sheets puff pastry (measuring
   15 cm x 25 cm), thawed if frozen
plain flour, for dusting
500 g desiree potatoes, peeled and
   chopped into large pieces
125 g unsalted butter
1 cup (250 ml) pouring cream
½ bunch chives, snipped
2 bunches asparagus, trimmed

CREPES
2 eggs
120 ml milk
15 g butter, melted
60 g plain flour
salt and pepper
small handful flat-leaf
   parsley, chopped
olive oil, for cooking

MUSHROOM STUFFING
30 g butter
1 golden shallot, diced
200 g button mushrooms, sliced
1 teaspoon chopped thyme
salt and pepper
1 small chicken breast fillet,
   skin removed
1 egg white
70 ml cream

1 With a very sharp knife, carefully cut the beef fillet in half lengthways. Wrap each piece tightly in plastic film and roll into a cylinder. Refrigerate for about an hour to 'set' the shape.

2 Next, prepare the crepes. Place the eggs, milk and melted butter in a bowl and stir to combine. Slowly whisk in the flour, season, then stir through the parsley and set the mixture aside to rest for 20 minutes.

3 Heat some oil in a 25 cm non-stick frying pan over medium heat. Pour in a third of the crepe mixture and tilt the pan so that the mixture evenly covers the base. Cook for 1 minute, then carefully flip the crepe with a spatula and cook the other side for 1–2 minutes or until golden. Transfer the cooked crepe to a plate and set aside to cool, then continue with the rest of the mixture, making three crepes in all. Store the cooked crepes in the fridge until ready to use.

4 Meanwhile, start on the mushroom stuffing. Melt the butter in a saucepan over medium heat, add the shallot and cook for 2 minutes or until soft. Add the mushrooms to the pan and cook for 4–5 minutes, then add the thyme and some salt and pepper and stir through. Remove the pan from the heat and leave the mixture to cool. Once cooled, transfer the mixture to a board and chop finely, then set aside in a bowl.

5 Place the chicken breast fillet in a food processor, season well and blend for 1 minute. Add the egg white and blend for 30 seconds, then add the cream and blend just until incorporated. Transfer this mixture to the bowl with the mushroom mix and stir through, then set aside.

6 Preheat the oven to 200°C and line a large baking tray with a sheet of greaseproof paper.

7 Remove the beef pieces from the fridge, unwrap them and season them all over with salt and pepper. Heat some oil in a non-stick frying pan over high heat and cook the beef briefly on all sides to seal, then remove from the pan and set aside.

8 In a small bowl, beat the egg yolks with 1 teaspoon water and a pinch of salt.

9 To assemble, lay out two crepes on a clean benchtop so they overlap by 4–5 cm. Take a third of the mushroom mixture and spoon it down the centre of the crepes in a strip about 1 cm thick and 5–6 cm wide. Place the sealed beef pieces end to end along the mushroom strip on the crepe, then spread the remaining mushroom mix evenly over the beef. Carefully roll up the crepes to cover the beef entirely, cutting off any excess, then brush all over with eggwash.

10 Place one sheet of puff pastry on the prepared baking tray and brush all over with eggwash. Place the crepe parcel on top, seam-side down.

11 Take the second sheet of puff pastry and place on the benchtop. Lightly dust with flour then roll the lattice cutter over, gently pulling the pastry apart with your fingers to open out the holes. Lay this sheet of pastry over the crepe parcel, pressing down gently with the sides of your hands to mould it evenly. Press the edges to join and trim off any excess pastry. Brush all over with eggwash and refrigerate for 1 hour.

12 Transfer the Beef Wellington to the oven and cook for 15 minutes, then reduce the oven temperature to 180°C and cook for a further 30 minutes. Remove from the oven and set aside to rest for 10 minutes.

13 Meanwhile, cook the potato in plenty of boiling salted water for 10–15 minutes or until tender, then drain well. Add the butter and cream and mash well, then season to taste, garnish with snipped chives and set aside, keeping warm.

14 Cook the asparagus in plenty of boiling salted water for about 2–3 minutes or until tender.

15 Slice the Beef Wellington into four and serve with the asparagus and buttery mash alongside.

RETRO DINNER PARTY

SERVES 4

Transport your guests back to the 70s with this elegant feast. The terrine is fantastic, and the Beef Wellington will put a smile on everybody's face. Just make sure that your guests leave room for dessert – the strawberry shortcake is not to be missed.

Pork and Pistachio Terrine with Peach Chutney	**15**
< **Beef Wellington with Asparagus and Mash**	**126**
Strawberry Shortcake	**202**

ROAST PORK LOIN WITH JERUSALEM ARTICHOKE PUREE AND CARAMELISED PEARS

SERVES 6

This dish takes a bit of preparation, but the final result is well worth the effort – your guests will be blown away by this sophisticated take on an all-time favourite. The unique flavour of Jerusalem artichokes really lifts this dish and the caramelised pears add a lovely touch of sweetness.

2 tablespoons vegetable oil
1.2 kg pork loin, trimmed of excess fat, tied at 2.5 cm intervals with kitchen string to form a neat shape
2 bunches English spinach, trimmed
200 g thinly sliced prosciutto
25 g butter
1½ tablespoons caster sugar
2 Williams pears, halved, cored, and sliced

squeeze of lemon juice
chervil, to garnish
220 ml mustard sauce (see page 225), warmed

POTATO CAKE
120 g butter
3 large desiree potatoes, cut into 1.5 mm slices
salt and pepper

JERUSALEM ARTICHOKE PUREE
40 g butter
2 golden shallots, finely chopped
1 clove garlic, crushed
7 large Jerusalem artichokes, peeled and cut into 1 cm chunks
300 ml chicken stock (see page 222)
70 ml pouring cream
salt and pepper

1 For the Jerusalem artichoke puree, melt the butter over medium heat in a saucepan then add the shallots and garlic and cook, stirring occasionally, for 5 minutes or until softened. Add the Jerusalem artichoke and stock and bring to a simmer. Cover, reduce the heat to low and cook for 20 minutes or until the artichoke is tender. Strain, reserving the cooking liquid, and place the artichoke, along with the cream, in a blender or food processor. Blend to a smooth puree, adding some of the reserved cooking liquid if necessary. Season to taste then set aside.

2 Preheat the oven to 180°C. Heat the oil in a large heavy-based frying pan over medium–high heat, add the pork loin and cook, turning often, for 5–6 minutes or until browned all over. Set the pork aside on a chopping board and remove the string.

3 Meanwhile, bring a large saucepan of water to the boil, add the spinach and cook for 30 seconds or until wilted, then drain well. Run the spinach under cold water, then drain again and pat dry with a clean tea towel.

4 Lay the prosciutto slices out on a clean benchtop, overlapping them to form a rectangle large enough to completely enclose the pork. Open up the spinach leaves as best you can and place evenly over the pork loin to cover. Place the pork loin on one edge of the prosciutto rectangle and carefully roll up to enclose, then secure at 2.5 cm intervals with kitchen string and place in a roasting tin. Roast for 35–40 minutes or until the

pork is cooked but still a little pink in the middle. Remove from the oven, cover loosely with foil and set aside to rest for 10 minutes.

5 Meanwhile, to make the potato cake, clarify the butter by melting it in a small saucepan over low heat until the white milk solids start to separate and rise to the top. Remove from the heat and leave to stand for 10 minutes, then carefully strain away the milky sediment.

6 Neatly line a small non-stick ovenproof frying pan with potato slices, overlapping them slightly, then drizzle over some clarified butter and season. Repeat with the rest of the potato slices and butter, then press firmly down on top. Cook over medium heat for 6–7 minutes until lightly golden around the edges, then transfer to the oven and bake for 35 minutes. Keep warm until ready to serve.

7 Melt the 25 g butter in a non-stick frying pan over medium heat, then add the sugar and cook, stirring, for 3–4 minutes or until golden. Add the pear and a squeeze of lemon juice and cook, turning often, for 5–6 minutes or until the pear is light golden, then transfer to a bowl. Gently reheat the artichoke puree in a small saucepan.

8 Transfer the pork to a large chopping board and thickly slice. Garnish with chervil and accompany with the mustard sauce. Slide the potato cake onto the board, cut into wedges and season well with salt. Serve the puree and caramelised pears alongside.

VEAL HOLSTEIN WITH POACHED EGG

SERVES 4

Veal Holstein was very popular on restaurant menus in the 1960s and 1970s. I have resurrected it, but instead of the usual fried egg I use an elegant poached duck egg. The best place to find Tuscan kale is an Italian grocer, where it will probably be called cavolo nero. You can also find it at specialty greengrocers or farmers' markets.

4 × 220 g veal cutlets
2 cups (300 g) plain flour
salt and pepper
6 eggs
100 ml milk
2 cups (300 g) panko
   (Japanese breadcrumbs)

2 cups (500 ml) olive oil,
   plus extra for cooking
2 heads cavolo nero
   (Tuscan kale), trimmed
20 g butter, diced
100 ml bordelaise sauce (see page 225)
2 tablespoons sherry vinegar

1 tablespoon extra virgin olive oil
4 teaspoons capers
small handful chopped flat-leaf parsley
4 duck eggs
2 tablespoons white wine vinegar
8 white anchovies
lemon wedges, to serve

1 Preheat the oven to 120°C.

2 Place the veal cutlets between two pieces of plastic film and lightly flatten with a meat mallet until the meat and the bone are the same thickness.

3 Place the flour in a bowl and season with salt and pepper. In another bowl, whisk the eggs with the milk. Place the panko in a third bowl.

4 Working with one cutlet at a time, coat the veal in flour, then dip into the eggwash and press into the panko.

5 Pour oil into a large frying pan to a depth of 5 mm and heat over medium–high heat. Add the cutlets in batches and cook for 2–3 minutes on each side until golden brown. Remove and drain on paper towel, then place in the oven to keep warm while you cook the rest.

6 Meanwhile, heat a dash of oil with the butter in another frying pan and add the cavolo nero and some salt and pepper. Cook over medium heat until wilted, then drain and set aside.

7 In a small saucepan, warm the bordelaise sauce over low–medium heat, and just before serving stir through the sherry vinegar, extra virgin olive oil, capers and chopped parsley. Season to taste.

8 To poach the eggs, half-fill a deep frying pan or large saucepan with water and add the vinegar. Bring to the boil then reduce to a simmer until bubbles can just be seen rising. Break each egg into a cup, stir the water with a spoon to create a whirlpool then gently slip in the egg. Cook for 3–4 minutes or until just set.

9 Arrange some drained cavolo nero in the middle of each plate then place a veal cutlet on top. Finish with a poached egg and a drizzle of bordelaise sauce, then top with a couple of anchovies. Serve with lemon wedges.

ROAST LAMB RUMP WITH PEA, MINT, RED ONION AND FETA SALAD

SERVES 4

This lovely dinner dish can be thrown together pretty quickly and the simple Greek-style salad is the perfect accompaniment.

4 × 200 g lamb rumps
salt and pepper
1 tablespoon vegetable oil
1¼ cups (200 g) fresh peas
    (from 400 g peas in pods)

100 g rocket
100 g marinated feta, drained
    and crumbled
¼ red onion, very finely sliced
2 tablespoons finely shredded mint

2 pieces preserved lemon, rind only,
    rinsed and very thinly sliced
100 ml extra virgin olive oil
lemon juice, to taste

1 Preheat the oven to 180°C.

2 Season the lamb rumps with salt and pepper. Heat the oil in a large, ovenproof frying pan over medium–high heat, then add the lamb and sear for a couple of minutes on each side until browned. Transfer the pan to the oven and cook for about 15 minutes or until cooked but still pink in the middle.

3 Remove the meat from the oven, cover loosely with foil and set aside to rest for 10 minutes.

4 Bring plenty of salted water to the boil in a large saucepan, toss in the peas for 1 minute to blanch, then drain and refresh in iced water. Drain well again and transfer to a salad bowl, along with the rocket, feta, onion, shredded mint, preserved lemon and olive oil, and add lemon juice to taste. Toss together and season with salt and pepper.

5 Slice each lamb rump and serve with the salad alongside.

ANGELA'S SLOW-COOKED LAMB

SERVES 6–8

This lamb literally melts in your mouth, and the best part about this dish is you can just throw it in the oven mid-afternoon and get on with preparing your other courses. The first time our good friend Angela Potts cooked this for us, it became one of my all-time favourite lamb dishes.

---

1 x 2.2 kg bone-in lamb shoulder
olive oil, for rubbing
finely grated zest and juice of 1 lemon
salt and pepper
6 cloves garlic, cut in half
   (or quarters if they are large)
6 anchovies in oil, drained and
   cut in half

1 sprig fresh rosemary, leaves picked
200 ml extra virgin olive oil
300 ml white wine
1 kg kipfler potatoes, scrubbed
   and cut in half lengthways
16 cloves garlic
3 pieces preserved lemon, rind only,
   rinsed and finely chopped

½ bunch oregano, leaves picked,
   stalks reserved
2 cups (500 ml) chicken stock
   (see page 222)
150 ml olive oil
green salad, to serve

---

1 Preheat the oven to 200°C.

2 Using a small, sharp knife, score the fat of the lamb shoulder in a diamond pattern and make twelve 1 cm incisions. With your hands, rub some olive oil all over the meat then press the lemon zest on top and season generously with salt and pepper. Take half a clove of garlic, half an anchovy fillet and a few rosemary leaves, press together to form a bundle and stuff one of these little bundles into each incision. Sprinkle the leftover rosemary on top.

3 Place the meat in a large roasting tin, then pour over the 200 ml olive oil and the white wine.

4 Place the potatoes in a large baking dish with the garlic, preserved lemon and oregano stalks. Pour over the chicken stock and 150 ml olive oil.

5 Cook the meat and potatoes for 45 minutes, stirring the potatoes every now and then.

6 Remove the potatoes from the oven, cover and set them aside. Reduce the oven temperature to 130°C. Baste the meat with the juices from the tin, then cover it loosely with foil and return to the oven for a further 2½ hours or until the meat falls off the bone.

7 Once cooked, remove the meat from the oven and leave it to rest, covered, for 10 minutes before carving.

8 Meanwhile, uncover the potatoes, fish out the oregano stalks and sprinkle in the leaves. Reheat in the oven for about 10 minutes before serving with the carved meat and a green salad.

LAMB AND FETA FILO PIES

SERVES 8

Lamb and feta taste great together in these delicious Greek-influenced individual pies. Make sure you cook the meat for at least 2½ hours – it will just melt in your mouth.

1.5 kg lamb neck fillets, trimmed and
   cut into 2.5 cm pieces
2 onions, sliced
5 cloves garlic, finely chopped
1½ teaspoons ground fennel
2 pieces preserved lemon, rind only,
   rinsed and finely chopped

360 g butter
2 cups (500 ml) chicken stock
   (see page 222)
8 bay leaves
1 bunch silverbeet (Swiss chard),
   leaves removed from tough stems
300 g sheep's feta, crumbled

100 g pine nuts, toasted
12 sheets filo pastry,
   thawed if frozen

1 Preheat the oven to 150°C.

2 Combine the lamb, onion, garlic, fennel and preserved lemon in a bowl and mix together well. Spoon the mixture evenly into eight 1½ cup (375 ml) ovenproof dishes. Chop 160 g of the butter and divide this and the chicken stock among the dishes, add a bay leaf to each, then tightly cover with foil and bake for 2½ hours or until the meat is very tender.

3 Meanwhile, place the silverbeet leaves in a large saucepan of boiling salted water and cook, covered, for 5 minutes or until tender. Drain well and allow to cool. Using your hands, squeeze the silverbeet firmly to get rid of as much liquid as possible, then roughly chop it.

4 Clarify the remaining butter by melting it in a small saucepan over low heat until the white milk solids start to separate and rise to the top. Remove from the heat and leave to stand for 10 minutes, then carefully strain away the milky sediment and set the clarified butter aside.

5 Remove the dishes from the oven and increase the oven temperature to 180°C.

6 Divide the silverbeet, feta and pine nuts among the dishes and gently stir to combine.

7 Cut the filo sheets in half widthways to give you twenty-four pieces. Working with three pieces for each pie, brush each sheet with clarified butter, then loosely scrunch it with your hands and place over the top of each dish to cover the filling.

8 Return the dishes to the oven and bake for 15 minutes or until the pastry is golden brown, then serve the pies immediately.

DRY-AGED T-BONE WITH BEARNAISE SAUCE

SERVES 4

This bistro classic (pictured overleaf) is wonderful served simply with a fresh green salad and roast potatoes, or it's a great match for celeriac remoulade (page 174). Don't be put off by the bearnaise sauce – take it step by step and you'll master it in no time.

---

2 tablespoons olive oil
2 × 1.2 kg dry-aged T-bone steaks
salt and pepper
handful picked watercress
celeriac remoulade (see page 174),
    to serve

BEARNAISE SAUCE
300 g butter
1 golden shallot, sliced
25 ml white wine or chardonnay vinegar
50 ml white wine
1 bay leaf

1 sprig tarragon, leaves picked and
    chopped, stalks reserved
6 black peppercorns, crushed
2 egg yolks
salt and pepper

---

1 To make the bearnaise sauce, melt the butter in a small saucepan over low heat until the white milk solids start to separate and rise to the top. Remove the pan from the heat and leave to stand for 10 minutes, then carefully strain away the milky sediment.

2 Meanwhile, place the shallot, vinegar, white wine, bay leaf, tarragon stalks and crushed peppercorns into another saucepan, bring to the boil and boil for 1–2 minutes. Remove from the heat and strain, discarding the solids.

3 Pour the reduced vinegar into a small heatproof bowl that fits snugly over a pan of simmering water, and then slowly whisk in the egg yolks over low–medium heat until they have thickened and doubled in volume.

4 Remove the bowl from the heat and slowly add the clarified butter, whisking continuously to emulsify. Season and finish with the tarragon leaves.

5 Preheat the barbecue to its hottest setting or place a chargrill pan over high heat, and preheat the oven to 180°C.

6 Pour the olive oil over the steaks and season generously with salt and pepper. Grill the steaks for 3–5 minutes on one side until nicely charred, then turn over and repeat on the other side.

7 Transfer the steaks to a baking tray and place in the oven for 8–10 minutes, then remove and set aside to rest for 10 minutes.

8 Serve the steaks on a large platter with the bearnaise sauce, some watercress and celeriac remoulade.

BRAISED SHORT RIB WITH ROSTI, CARROTS AND LEEKS

SERVES 6

Start preparing this dish (pictured overleaf) the day before, so that you can leave the meat to marinate overnight. On the day of serving, leave yourself a good six hours to prepare the beef.

1 × 2.3 kg beef short rib in one piece, bones removed (ask your butcher to do this for you)
2 onions, coarsely chopped
2 carrots, coarsely chopped
1 leek, well washed, trimmed and coarsely chopped
2 stalks celery, coarsely chopped
2 cloves garlic, bruised
2 sprigs thyme
2 bay leaves
1.5 litres red wine
1.5 litres veal stock (see page 223)
½ cup (75 g) plain flour

⅓ cup (80 ml) vegetable oil
1 teaspoon black peppercorns
1 teaspoon juniper berries
600 g (about 2 large) potatoes (I like to use Sebago potatoes for this), peeled and grated
1 tablespoon salt
120 g butter
18 baby (Dutch) carrots, peeled and halved lengthways on the diagonal
18 pencil leeks, well washed and trimmed
large handful watercress sprigs

CRISP SHALLOTS
1 teaspoon smoked paprika
½ cup (75 g) plain flour
salt
100 ml milk
4 golden shallots, thinly sliced widthways
400 ml vegetable oil

1 Trim any excess fat and sinew off the beef, then place it in a large non-reactive bowl with the chopped vegetables, garlic cloves, herbs and red wine. Cover and refrigerate for 24 hours.

2 Preheat the oven to 170°C.

3 Take the bowl from the fridge and strain the red wine into a saucepan, reserving the vegetables and beef. Bring the wine to the boil and cook over medium–high heat for 10 minutes or until reduced slightly, then add the stock. Bring to a simmer, then reduce the heat to low and keep warm while you prepare the beef and vegetables.

4 Lightly coat the beef in flour, shaking off the excess.

5 Heat half the oil over medium heat in a large frying pan, add the reserved vegetables and cook, stirring often, for 10 minutes or until golden, then transfer to a roasting tin.

6 Heat the remaining oil over medium heat in the pan, add the beef and cook for 3 minutes on each side or until golden. Transfer to the roasting tin and add the peppercorns and juniper berries. Pour over the stock, then cover the dish tightly with foil and cook in the oven for 3 hours or until the beef is tender.

7 Once cooked, carefully remove the meat from the roasting tin and transfer to a chopping board to cool. Place another board on top of the meat to weigh it down, then refrigerate for 2 hours or until chilled. Strain the cooking liquid into a saucepan, discarding the solids, and skim off any fat from the top before bringing to the boil over high heat. Reduce the heat to medium and simmer for 20 minutes or until reduced and thickened slightly, then set the sauce aside.

8 Meanwhile, combine the grated potato and salt in a colander and leave to stand for 5 minutes to drain. Using your hands, squeeze out as much excess liquid as possible, then dry the potato with paper towel and form into neat rounds about 7 cm in diameter.

9 Clarify the butter by melting it in a small saucepan over low heat until the white milk solids start to separate and rise to the top. Remove the pan from the heat and leave to stand for 10 minutes, then carefully strain away the milky sediment.

10 Heat the clarified butter in a large non-stick frying pan over medium heat. Working in batches, fry the potato rounds for 3–4 minutes each side until golden and crisp, adding more butter to the pan as necessary. Remove from the pan, drain on paper towel and keep warm.

11 To make the crisp shallots, mix the paprika with the flour in a bowl and season with a little salt. Pour the milk into a separate bowl. Toss the sliced shallots in the milk, then the flour, shaking off any excess.

12 Heat the oil in a saucepan to 140°C or until a cube of bread turns golden in 25 seconds, then fry the shallots for 4 minutes or until golden and crisp. Remove with a slotted spoon then drain on paper towel.

13 Gently reheat the sauce. Cut the meat into twelve even pieces, then carefully place these in the sauce and heat through.

14 Bring a large saucepan of salted water to the boil, add the carrot and leeks and cook for 4 minutes or until just tender, then drain well.

15 Divide the meat among six plates then scatter some crisp shallots on top. Arrange two or three pieces of potato rosti around the meat, along with some carrot and leek. Spoon over some sauce and garnish with watercress before serving.

FRENCH-THEMED DINNER PARTY

SERVES 6

Everybody loves French food, and your guests will feel very special when you prepare this Gallic feast for them. If you like, you can go the whole hog – red-and-white checked tablecloth, candles in bottles, Edith Piaf playing in the background – you get the picture. The hearty bouillabaisse is a nice foil to the braised short rib, and the chocolate fondants will have your guests begging for more.

Cod Brandade with Mussels	20
Bouillabaisse	37
< Braised Short Rib with Rosti, Carrots and Leeks	142
Chocolate Fondants with Raspberries and Vanilla Ice Cream	212

LAMB QUESADILLAS

SERVES 4

These quesadillas are just right for a laidback dinner with family or friends, with everyone digging in and piling their plates high. The ras el hanout (see recipe on page 36) and harissa add a bit of bite. You could also serve the avocado salsa on its own as a dip.

4 roma tomatoes
olive oil, for cooking
1 brown onion, finely diced
2 cloves garlic, finely diced
500 g lamb mince
2 tablespoons harissa
1 tablespoon ras el hanout
    (see page 36)
½ bunch coriander, leaves
    roughly chopped

olive oil spray
8 tortillas
200 g mozzarella, grated
200 g sour cream
lemon and lime cheeks, to serve
baby coriander or regular coriander,
    to serve

AVOCADO SALSA
2 avocados, finely diced
1 red onion, finely diced
1 bunch coriander, leaves
    finely chopped
1 teaspoon ground cumin
juice of 1 lime, or to taste
20 ml olive oil
salt and pepper

1 Use a small, sharp knife to cut a cross in the base of each tomato. Bring plenty of salted water to the boil in a large saucepan. Add the tomatoes and blanch for about 30 seconds, then remove with a slotted spoon and transfer to a bowl of iced water. Drain well, then peel the tomatoes and cut into quarters. Remove the seeds and finely dice the flesh.

2 Combine half the diced tomato with all the salsa ingredients in a bowl. Taste and adjust seasoning if required, then set aside.

3 Preheat the oven to 200°C.

4 Heat some oil in a large heavy-based frying pan over medium heat then add the onion and garlic and cook for 2–3 minutes or until softened but not coloured. Add the lamb mince and cook for 5–10 minutes or until browned. Add the harissa and ras el hanout and cook for 5 minutes.

5 Transfer the lamb mixture to a sieve and drain away the excess oil. Leave to cool, then place in a large bowl and mix in the rest of the diced tomato and the chopped coriander.

6 Spray a pizza tray with oil and line with a tortilla. Spoon over a quarter of the lamb mixture and top with a quarter of the grated mozzarella. Place the other tortilla on top, pressing firmly to enclose, then spray with more oil. Assemble the other quesadillas and, working in batches if necessary, transfer them to the oven to bake for 5 minutes. Remove the trays from the oven, flip the quesadillas over with a spatula and cook for 5 minutes on the other side, or until golden brown and crispy.

7 Cut each quesadilla into four and garnish with some coriander, then serve with lemon and lime cheeks, sour cream and the avocado salsa.

RACK OF LAMB WITH WILD MUSHROOMS, FONDANT POTATOES AND TRUFFLE AIOLI

SERVES 6

Rack of lamb is always a treat, and this is a stunning dish. The fondant potatoes just melt in your mouth. I like to use a mixture of cepes and fly caps for this recipe, but if you can't find these, substitute Swiss browns or button mushrooms. You can buy truffle oil from specialty grocers and some supermarkets.

6 x 4-bone lamb racks, boned and
　　fat trimmed (ask your butcher to
　　do this for you)
2 tablespoons olive oil
50 g butter
250 g mixed wild mushrooms, sliced
1 tablespoon truffle oil
½ clove garlic, finely chopped
2 tablespoons chopped flat-leaf parsley
salt and pepper

1 bunch English spinach, trimmed,
　　well washed and drained
90 ml lamb jus (see page 225)
handful picked thyme leaves, to serve

FONDANT POTATOES
250 g butter, softened
6 desiree potatoes, peeled
　　and trimmed into
　　6 cm × 3 cm cylinders
salt

TRUFFLE AIOLI
2 egg yolks
1 teaspoon Dijon mustard
3 teaspoons white wine vinegar
½ clove garlic
lemon juice, to taste
200 ml olive oil
2½ tablespoons truffle oil
salt and pepper

1 To make the fondant potatoes, spread the butter over the base of a large saucepan. Place the potato cylinders on top of the butter – they should fit snugly in the pan but must not touch each other. Season with salt and pour in just enough water to cover the potatoes. Cut out a round of baking paper large enough to fit the pan, butter it and place it on top of the potatoes. Bring to the boil, then reduce the heat and simmer until all the water and butter have been absorbed and the potatoes have caramelised; this should take about 30–40 minutes. Don't shake the pan while the potatoes are cooking as this will hinder the caramelisation. Check that the potatoes are cooked by inserting a skewer through the centre; it may be necessary to add more water so that the butter does not burn. Remove from the heat and leave to cool, then transfer the potato cylinders to a baking tray and set aside.

2 Meanwhile, for the truffle aioli, combine the egg yolks, mustard, vinegar, garlic and a squeeze of lemon juice in a bowl and whisk to combine well. Whisking continuously, add the oils in a slow, steady stream until thick and emulsified – take care not to add them too quickly or the mayonnaise will 'break'. Season to taste, adding a little more lemon juice if necessary.

3 Preheat the oven to 200°C.

4 Heat the olive oil in a large, ovenproof frying pan over medium–high heat, add the lamb and cook, turning once, for 4 minutes or until golden. Transfer the pan to the oven and cook for 5 minutes or until the meat is cooked but still a little pink in the middle. Cover the pan loosely with foil and rest the lamb for 10 minutes before serving. Place the fondant potatoes in the oven to warm through before serving.

5 Melt the butter in a frying pan over medium heat, add the mushrooms and cook, stirring often, for 3–4 minutes or until tender. Add the truffle oil, garlic and parsley and season to taste. Transfer to a plate and set aside.

6 Wipe out the pan, add a splash of oil and return it to the stove over medium–high heat. Add the spinach, cover and cook, shaking the pan, for 2–3 minutes or until the spinach has wilted. Heat the jus in a small saucepan.

7 Slice each piece of lamb widthways into three even-sized pieces and transfer to serving plates, with a fondant potato alongside. Divide the spinach between the plates and top with some mushrooms, then drizzle with aioli and garnish with thyme leaves. Pour the hot lamb jus over just before serving.

STEAK AND KIDNEY PUDDINGS WITH SAUTEED CABBAGE

SERVES 6

My version of the hearty English classic – this is a winner as a family meal or for entertaining. I use beef brisket, a boneless cut from the breast or lower chest, because it has more flavour than other cuts. You'll probably need to order the suet from your butcher in advance. The sauteed cabbage is a versatile side dish, particularly good for winter entertaining.

350 g beef brisket, trimmed and cut
    into 1 cm pieces
350 g beef kidneys, trimmed and cut
    into 1 cm pieces
2½ tablespoons plain flour
150 ml warm veal stock (see page 223)
3 teaspoons Vegemite or other
    yeast spread
2 tablespoons hot English mustard
2½ tablespoons Worcestershire sauce
½ onion, finely chopped
salt and pepper
50 g butter, softened

1 egg, beaten
800 g desiree potatoes,
    peeled and cut into chunks
75 g unsalted butter
¾ cup (180 ml) pouring cream

SUET PASTRY
500 g self-raising flour
2 teaspoons salt
1 teaspoon freshly ground black pepper
200 g fresh beef suet, grated (ask your
    butcher to do this for you)

SAUTEED CABBAGE
1 carrot, cut into thin batons
1 small head celeriac (about 200 g),
    peeled and cut into thin batons
30 g duck fat or butter
150 g piece smoked bacon,
    rind removed and cut into small,
    thin strips
1 clove garlic, crushed
400 g Savoy cabbage (about ½ a small
    cabbage), tough outer leaves and
    core removed, remaining leaves
    cut into thick strips

1 To make the pastry, sift the flour into a bowl and add the salt and pepper. Using your hands, rub in the suet to combine well. Gradually add about 1½ cups (375 ml) cold water and mix in with your hands until the dough is firm (you may need to use more or less water depending on the consistency of the flour). Turn the dough out onto a lightly floured benchtop, knead until smooth then wrap in plastic film and rest at room temperature while you prepare the filling.

2 In a bowl, combine the brisket and kidneys with the flour until the flour coats the meat. In another bowl mix the stock, Vegemite, mustard and Worcestershire sauce and whisk to combine well. Add the onion and season to taste, then add this to the meat mixture and combine.

3 Grease six 375 ml heatproof pudding bowls with the softened butter.

4 Take two-thirds of the pastry, divide into six equal pieces and roll each piece into a round large enough to line the pudding bowls. Lay the rounds in the bowls, then divide the meat mixture among the bowls and brush some beaten egg around the exposed lip of the pastry. Divide the remaining third of pastry into six even pieces and roll each piece into a round large enough to cover the pudding bowls. Place the pastry lids on top and press firmly to seal the edges well, trimming off any excess.

5 Place the pudding bowls in a large saucepan or stockpot (you may need to use two saucepans if you don't have one large enough to fit them all) and add enough water to come halfway up the side of the bowls. Cover, bring to a simmer and cook over medium heat for 2 hours.

6 Meanwhile, for the sauteed cabbage, cook the carrot and celeriac in a saucepan of boiling salted water for 2 minutes or until softened, then drain well and set aside.

7 Heat the duck fat and bacon in a large saucepan over medium heat and cook, stirring, for 5 minutes or until the duck fat has melted. Add the garlic and cabbage, stir to combine then cover and cook over low–medium heat, stirring occasionally, for 8–10 minutes or until softened. Add the carrot and celeriac, stir to combine then cover and cook for another 3–4 minutes or until the vegetables are soft. Season to taste, set aside and keep warm.

8 Cook the potato in plenty of boiling salted water for 10–15 minutes or until tender, then drain well. Add the cream and butter and mash well, then season to taste, set aside and keep warm.

9 Carefully unmould the puddings by inverting the bowls onto plates then serve straightaway with plenty of mash and sauteed cabbage.

BRAISED BEEF CHEEKS WITH PICKLED BEETROOT

SERVES 6

Beef cheeks are lean cuts of beef, which, when slow-cooked, are remarkably tender. The combination of honey and vinegar give this dish a great sweet-and-sour taste. You may as well pickle the whole bunch of beetroot – you will need about three for this recipe, but you can store the rest in a sterilised jar (see page 13) in the fridge for 2–3 weeks.

---

100 ml vegetable oil
2 onions, coarsely chopped
2 carrots, coarsely chopped
1.2 kg beef cheeks
½ cup (75 g) plain flour
3 tablespoons honey
½ cup (125 ml) sherry vinegar
1 teaspoon cloves

4 sprigs thyme
2 bay leaves
1 litre chicken or veal stock
   (see page 222–3)
1 bunch beetroot, leaves reserved
   to garnish
pickling liquid (see page 17),
   to cover

MUSTARD CREME FRAICHE
250 g creme fraiche
2 tablespoons seeded mustard
1 tablespoon hot English mustard
salt and pepper

---

1 Preheat the oven to 150°C.

2 Heat half the oil in a large frying pan over medium heat, add the onion and carrot and cook, stirring often, for 10–15 minutes or until golden, then transfer to a large casserole.

3 Dust the beef cheeks in the flour, shaking off the excess and season well with salt and pepper. Heat the remaining oil in the frying pan, then cook the beef cheeks over medium heat for 3–4 minutes on each side or until golden. Transfer to the casserole with the vegetables.

4 Add the honey and vinegar to the pan and cook, stirring to dislodge any stuck-on bits, for 1–2 minutes, then add this to the casserole along with the cloves, herbs and stock. Place the casserole over medium heat and bring the mixture to a simmer, then cover and transfer to the oven. Cook for 3 hours or until the meat is very tender.

5 Meanwhile, place the beetroot in a saucepan, cover with pickling liquid and bring to a boil. Cook over medium heat for 30–40 minutes or until tender, then drain. When the beetroot are cool enough to handle, peel off the skins, then cut into wedges, reserving one whole beetroot to make a puree. Set the wedges aside and keep warm.

6 Once the meat is cooked, remove it from the casserole with a slotted spoon and set aside, keeping warm. Strain the liquid into a saucepan, discarding the solids, and skim off the fat from the surface. Bring the liquid to a boil, then simmer for 25 minutes or until reduced and thickened slightly.

7 Transfer the whole beetroot to a blender or food processor and pulse until smooth, then cover and keep warm.

8 Meanwhile, place the creme fraiche and the mustards in a bowl and season with salt and pepper. Whisk together until the mixture thickens and resembles whipped cream.

9 To serve, divide the meat between six plates and arrange a few beetroot wedges around the meat. Dollop some beetroot puree on the plates and scatter a few beetroot leaves on top. Serve a spoonful of mustard creme fraiche alongside, and drizzle some reduced sauce over the meat to finish.

STICKY PORK RIBS

SERVES 4

Everybody loves pork ribs – your guests will be licking their fingers and demanding seconds. Serve these with a potato salad and coleslaw.

---

2 kg baby back pork ribs, in one piece
2 litres chicken stock (see page 222)
1 brown onion, roughly chopped
2 bay leaves

3 sprigs thyme
1 teaspoon black peppercorns
salt and pepper
1 cup (250 ml) tomato sauce

1 tablespoon hot English mustard
3 tablespoons Worcestershire sauce
2 tablespoons honey
1 tablespoon malt vinegar

---

1 Place the pork ribs in a large heavy-based saucepan or casserole, cover with the chicken stock then toss in the onion, bay leaves, thyme and peppercorns. Season with salt and pepper, bring to a simmer then cook over low heat for 1 hour or until the meat is falling off the bone.

2 Meanwhile, preheat the oven to 180°C.

3 Combine the tomato sauce, mustard, Worcestershire sauce, honey and vinegar in a bowl and season with salt and pepper.

4 Once the ribs are ready, carefully lift them from the stock, taking care to keep them intact, and transfer them to an oven tray. Brush them all over with the tomato sauce mixture, then place them in the oven to bake for about 20–30 minutes, removing them every 5 minutes or so to re-apply the glaze, until the ribs are sticky and browned all over.

5 Remove the tray from the oven, cut the meat into individual ribs and serve immediately.

CRUMBED LAMB CUTLETS WITH ANCHOVY BUTTER SAUCE AND PICKLED SHALLOT AND WATERCRESS SALAD

SERVES 6

Crumbed cutlets bring back happy childhood memories but, instead of the usual peas and mash, I have dressed them up for this very adult version with a rich sauce and a flavoursome salad. Just note that you need to prepare the pickled shallots the day before.

⅔ cup (100 g) flour, seasoned
    with salt and pepper
3 eggs
2½ tablespoons milk
2 cups (140 g) panko (Japanese
    breadcrumbs)
12 lamb cutlets
3 tablespoons vegetable oil
1 bunch watercress
2½ tablespoons extra virgin olive oil

PICKLED SHALLOT
300 g golden shallots, finely sliced
1½ tablespoons salt
½ cup (125 ml) rice wine vinegar
⅓ cup (75 g) caster sugar
6 cloves
2 teaspoons brown mustard seeds
½ teaspoon black peppercorns
1 × 2.5 cm piece ginger, sliced
1 red chilli, split in half lengthways
⅓ cup (80 ml) chardonnay vinegar
1 clove garlic, bruised

ANCHOVY BUTTER SAUCE
125 g butter
12 anchovy fillets, roughly chopped
2 tablespoons salted capers, rinsed
1 small lemon, peeled, all white pith
    removed, segmented and chopped
1½ tablespoons chopped
    flat-leaf parsley
1½ tablespoons extra virgin olive oil

1 For the pickled shallot, toss together the sliced shallot and 1 tablespoon of the salt in a bowl, then leave to stand at room temperature for 2 hours. Rinse well, then gently squeeze to remove any excess liquid. Set aside in a bowl. Place the remaining ingredients with ½ tablespoon salt and 300 ml water in a small saucepan and bring to the boil, then reduce the heat to low and simmer for 20 minutes. Strain, discarding the solids, then pour over the shallot. Cool to room temperature then cover with plastic film and refrigerate for 24 hours. Bring to room temperature before using.

2 Place the seasoned flour in a bowl. Combine the eggs and milk in another bowl and whisk to combine well. Place the panko in a third bowl. Lightly dust the cutlets in the flour, shaking off any excess. Dip each cutlet in the egg mixture, draining off the excess, then place in the panko, pressing firmly so the cutlets are well coated.

3 Heat half the vegetable oil in a large, heavy-based frying pan over medium heat, add half the cutlets and cook, turning once, for 8 minutes or until cooked through but still a little pink on the inside. Remove to a warmed plate and cover loosely with foil, then repeat with the remaining oil and cutlets.

4 Meanwhile, for the anchovy butter, melt the butter in a small saucepan until it starts to foam, then add the anchovies, capers, lemon, parsley and olive oil and swirl to combine.

5 Drain the pickled shallot and combine in a bowl with the watercress and extra virgin olive oil. Divide the cutlets and salad among six plates, and spoon the anchovy butter sauce over and around the cutlets. Serve immediately.

LAMB TAGINE

SERVES 4–6

This Moroccan stew is wonderful on a cold winter's night with a good glass of red. For best results, make sure you allow the full three-hour cooking time. This is great served with other dishes as part of a Middle-Eastern feast, with everyone helping themselves.

100 ml vegetable oil
1.2 kg lamb neck fillets, trimmed,
    cut into 3 cm pieces
salt and pepper
2 onions, thinly sliced
6 cloves garlic
100 g raisins
2 cinnamon sticks
3 blades mace

3 teaspoons ground cumin
2 teaspoons ground coriander
2 pieces preserved lemon, rind only,
    rinsed and chopped
1 tablespoon harissa
2 × 400 g cans chopped tomatoes
3 cups (750 ml) chicken stock
    (see page 222)
1¼ cups (250 g) instant couscous

25 g butter, chopped
1 tablespoon chopped flat-leaf parsley
3 tablespoons Greek-style yoghurt
½ red onion, thinly sliced
1 tablespoon chopped coriander leaves
salt and pepper

1 Heat half the oil in a large heavy-based frying pan and, working in batches, brown the lamb over medium–high heat. Season to taste then set aside.

2 Heat the remaining oil in a large heavy-based saucepan over medium heat, add the onions and garlic cloves and cook, stirring occasionally, for 8 minutes or until the onions start to turn golden. Add the raisins, spices, preserved lemon and harissa and cook, stirring, for 1–2 minutes or until fragrant. Add the browned lamb, tomato and 2 cups (500 ml) of the stock and stir to combine well. Bring the mixture to a simmer, cover and cook over low heat for 3 hours or until the lamb is very tender.

3 Place the couscous in a large heatproof bowl. Bring the remaining stock to the boil in a small saucepan then pour it over the couscous. Add the chopped butter and stir through, then cover the bowl with plastic film and leave for 5 minutes to absorb.

4 Season to taste and stir through the parsley, then dollop the yoghurt on top and scatter with the thinly sliced onion and coriander leaves.

5 Serve the tagine and couscous at the table and let everyone help themselves.

WAGYU BEEF BURGERS WITH TOMATO CHUTNEY

SERVES 6

This upmarket version of the traditional hamburger is great served with a beer after a day at the beach. A word of warning – you need to prepare the dill pickles a week in advance so that they have time to mature. The recipe for tomato chutney makes 1 litre. Transfer what you don't use into sterilised jars (see page 13), seal immediately, then store in the fridge for up to 2 months. The chutney can be served as a dip, or with roast pork, cold meats and even breakfast sausages for a special treat.

1 large beetroot, washed and trimmed
pickling liquid (see page 17), to cover
vegetable oil, for cooking
6 seeded bread rolls
small handful rocket leaves
6 slices Beaufort cheese
12 slices tomato

BEEF PATTIES
1 kg wagyu beef mince
1 onion, finely chopped
¼ bunch flat-leaf parsley,
   roughly chopped

1 red chilli, finely chopped
2 tablespoons tomato sauce
1 tablespoon Worcestershire sauce
1 teaspoon salt
½ teaspoon pepper

DILL PICKLES
1 kg Lebanese (small) cucumbers,
   cut into 5 mm thick slices
1 tablespoon salt
1 bunch dill, finely chopped
2 cups (500 ml) white wine vinegar
100 g caster sugar

TOMATO CHUTNEY
2 kg roma tomatoes
50 ml extra virgin olive oil
1 red onion, finely chopped
100 g caster sugar
50 ml red wine vinegar
salt and pepper

1 To prepare the dill pickles, place the cucumber slices in a bowl with the salt and leave for about 15 minutes to draw out excess moisture. Wash off the salt then pat the cucumber dry with paper towel.

2 Mix the cucumber with the chopped dill, vinegar and sugar, and place in a 1 litre preserving jar. Store in the fridge for 1 week before using.

3 To prepare the tomato chutney, use a small, sharp knife to cut a cross in the base of each tomato. Bring plenty of salted water to the boil in a large saucepan. Add the tomatoes and blanch for about 30 seconds, then remove with a slotted spoon and transfer to a bowl of iced water. Drain well, then peel the tomatoes and chop the flesh.

4 Heat the oil in a saucepan over medium heat and cook the onion until translucent. Add the sugar and cook, stirring occasionally, for 7–8 minutes or until the mixture starts to caramelise. Pour in the vinegar and stir to dislodge any stuck-on bits from the base of the pan. Add the chopped tomato and season to taste, then simmer for about 40 minutes until the chutney has thickened. Remove from the heat and set aside.

5 Place the whole beetroot in a saucepan and cover with pickling liquid. Cook over medium–high heat for 20–30 minutes or until softened. Leave to cool in the liquid, then remove and rub off the skin with your fingers. Slice and set aside.

6 To prepare the burger patties, mix together all the ingredients with your hands in a large bowl until well combined. Divide into six even portions and shape into patties.

7 Heat a large frying pan over medium–high heat. Lightly brush the patties all over with vegetable oil, then fry for 3–4 minutes each side or until browned and cooked through.

8 While the patties are cooking, split the bread rolls in half and lightly toast under the oven grill.

9 To assemble the burgers, place a couple of rocket leaves and a few slices of pickled beetroot onto the toasted roll, followed by some dill pickle. Lay a burger patty on top, then a slice of cheese and a spoonful of tomato chutney. Top with two slices of tomato and the other half of the toasted roll, and serve with extra tomato chutney on the side.

SALADS AND VEGETABLES

ZUCCHINI FLOWERS WITH RICOTTA, PINE NUTS AND BASIL

SERVES 4

This dish, which is very popular in Italy, can be served on its own as an appetiser, or as an accompaniment to a main course. Make sure you use cold salted butter – it helps create the lovely nutty brown foam that you want here.

1½ tablespoons pine nuts
6 basil leaves, shredded
1 cup (250 g) fresh ricotta

salt and pepper
12 zucchini flowers, stamens removed
olive oil

50 g cold salted butter
50 g muscatel raisins
1 tablespoon lemon juice, or to taste

---

1 Toast the pine nuts by tossing them in a dry frying pan over medium heat for a minute or two until golden. Remove and set aside.

2 In a small bowl, mix half of the shredded basil with the ricotta and season with salt and pepper. Using a piping bag or teaspoon, half-fill each flower with some mixture then gently twist the ends of the flowers to form a seal. Sprinkle a little olive oil over the stuffed flowers then season with salt and pepper.

3 Bring a large saucepan of water to the boil. Place the flowers in a steamer insert and place this in the saucepan. Cover and steam for 4 minutes, then carefully remove from the steamer and set aside on a plate.

4 Heat the butter in a small saucepan over medium heat until golden and foaming. Add the toasted pine nuts, raisins, lemon juice and the remaining basil and stir to combine.

5 Arrange the zucchini flowers on a large platter and spoon the butter mixture over.

SALAD OF CRAB AND WITLOF WITH MANGO MAYONNAISE

SERVES 4

This combination is hard to beat for a light summer's dinner. Crab is such a luxury, and I think the less you do with it the better (I've used Alaskan crab, which is available from specialty fishmongers). Here it is accompanied by a tangy mayonnaise and a fantastic salad. You could substitute prawns for a variation on the theme.

---

1 large mango, halved, stone removed
1 tablespoon sherry vinegar
75 ml olive oil
75 ml grapeseed oil
salt and pepper
4 tomatoes, cut into quarters, seeds
   removed and flesh cut into strips

½ large ripe avocado, peeled
   and thinly sliced
200 g cooked Alaskan crab meat
¼ bunch mint, leaves picked
¼ bunch basil, leaves picked
½ bunch chives, snipped
handful frisee (curly endive) leaves

2 punnets mache (lambs' lettuce)
4 witlof (chicory), trimmed
   and leaves separated

---

1 Scoop out the flesh from one half of the mango and place in the bowl of a food processor, along with the sherry vinegar, oils and salt and pepper to taste. Blend to a smooth puree then set aside.

2 Cut the flesh from the other mango half into small pieces and transfer to a large bowl. Add the tomato, avocado, crab meat, herbs and salad leaves and toss gently to combine.

3 Drizzle the mango mayonnaise over the salad, season with salt and pepper and toss again before serving.

LOBSTER SALAD WITH TOMATO AND LIME DRESSING

SERVES 4–6

The rich flavour of the lobster in this stunning dish is set off to perfection by the tangy dressing and the slightly sweet taste of the semi-dried tomatoes. Great served with a glass of chilled champagne.

1 × 800 g whole lobster, cooked
1 teaspoon finely grated lime zest
1½ tablespoons good-quality
   egg mayonnaise
salt and pepper
1 bunch thin asparagus, trimmed
2 radishes, trimmed and sliced
   into very thin rounds
1 lime, rind and all white pith removed,
   flesh cut into segments
small handful watercress

SEMI-DRIED TOMATOES
200 g rock salt
250 g baby roma tomatoes,
   cut in half lengthways
½ teaspoon sea salt
1½ tablespoons olive oil

TOMATO AND LIME DRESSING
250 g very ripe vine-ripened tomatoes,
   roughly chopped
small handful basil leaves
1 teaspoon salt
¼ teaspoon freshly ground black pepper
2 teaspoons caster sugar
¼ cup (60 ml) lime juice
75 ml tomato juice
1 tablespoon olive oil
1 tablespoon grapeseed oil

1 To make the semi-dried tomatoes, preheat the oven to 100°C and line a baking tray with the rock salt.

2 Arrange the tomatoes on the tray, skin-side down, sprinkle with sea salt, drizzle over the olive oil and bake for 40 minutes or until shrivelled slightly. Remove from the oven and set aside.

3 For the dressing, combine the chopped tomato with the basil, salt, pepper, sugar, lime juice and tomato juice in a food processor or blender and process to a smooth puree. Set aside for 20 minutes to allow the flavours to infuse.

4 Transfer the puree to a large piece of clean muslin, bring the edges together and secure with a strong rubber band or some string. Hang the bag over a bowl or plastic container so that the juices drip into the bowl – do not press on the bag or the juices will be cloudy. Leave for several hours or until you have about 200 ml strained juice, then discard the leftover puree in the bag. Add the olive oil and grapeseed oil to the strained juice and transfer the bowl of dressing to the fridge to chill while you prepare the lobster.

5 Slice the lobster tail in half lengthways then remove the shell and intestinal tract. Cut off any ragged pieces of meat from the end of the tail, finely dice and transfer to a bowl. Add the lime zest and mayonnaise to the bowl and stir through, season and set aside.

6 Cut the rest of the lobster meat into bite-sized pieces and set aside.

7 Blanch the asparagus in plenty of boiling salted water for 2–3 minutes, then drain and cut into short lengths.

8 Arrange the lobster meat, asparagus, radish, lime segments, some semi-dried tomatoes and watercress onto plates and spoon over dollops of lobster mayonnaise. Drizzle over the dressing just before serving.

SQUAB SALAD WITH LENTIL VINAIGRETTE

SERVES 4

A squab is a young pigeon, which tastes particularly tender and is a real delicacy. You'll need to order this in advance from a specialty butcher. You could substitute duck breast, if you prefer. As the squab legs can be tough, rather than serving them you could save them to use later for making a stock, soup or sauce. I really love the combination of bacon, grapes and lentils in the salad too.

½ cup (100 g) brown lentils,
    well washed
150 g smoked bacon or speck,
    rind removed and reserved,
    meat cut into 2 cm long batons
1 bay leaf
2 sprigs thyme
1 clove garlic, crushed

1 cup (250 ml) chicken stock
    (see page 222)
4 squabs
salt and pepper
olive oil, for pan-frying and dressing
25 g butter
100 g white grapes, cut in half
100 ml chicken jus (see page 224)

2½ tablespoons balsamic vinegar
1 tablespoon chopped flat-leaf parsley
handful baby mache (lambs' lettuce)
handful frisee (curly endive),
    leaves picked
handful red coral lettuce

1 Place the lentils in a saucepan with the bacon rind, bay leaf, thyme and garlic. Cover with the stock and bring to the boil, then reduce the heat to low and simmer for 20 minutes or until the lentils are just tender. Take the pan off the heat and leave the lentils to cool in the liquid.

2 Using a boning knife, remove the breast fillets from the squab, leaving the skin on and season with salt and pepper.

3 Heat a little olive oil in a large frying pan. Place the squab breasts in the pan, skin-side down, and cook for 2 minutes. Turn them over and add 20 g butter, then cook for a further 2 minutes. Remove the breasts from the pan, loosely cover with foil and set aside to rest.

4 Wipe out the pan and place over medium heat. Add the bacon and cook, stirring, for 4–5 minutes or until golden.

5 Drain the lentils, discarding the rind, herbs and garlic. Add the lentils and grapes to the pan with the bacon or speck, then stir in the jus and vinegar. Bring to the boil, then reduce the heat and simmer for about 1 minute. Add the remaining butter and swirl the pan so the butter is incorporated into the sauce. Add the parsley, season with salt and pepper, then remove the pan from the heat and cover to keep warm.

6 Dress the salad leaves with a little olive oil and arrange on serving plates. Carve each squab breast into three pieces and place on the salad leaves. Spoon the lentil vinaigrette around and serve.

CABBAGE STUFFED WITH BACON AND PRUNES

SERVES 4

Savoy cabbage, which comes from the Savoy region on the borders of France, Italy and Switzerland, has the sweetest flavour of any cabbage. This works well as a light main course.

---

1 Savoy cabbage
olive oil, for greasing
50 g butter
1 onion, finely chopped
2 cloves garlic, finely chopped
salt and pepper

½ cup (105 g) pitted chopped prunes
100 g rindless smoked bacon,
   roughly chopped
1 bunch sage, leaves picked and
   roughly chopped
1 tablespoon chopped thyme

500 g minced pork
1 teaspoon ground allspice

---

1 Remove the large, dark green outer leaves from the cabbage and set aside. Cut out the core and finely shred the rest of the cabbage, transfer to a bowl and set aside.

2 Lightly grease a 2 litre heatproof glass or ceramic bowl with a little olive oil.

3 Bring a large saucepan of salted water to the boil, add the whole cabbage leaves and cook for 3 minutes or until just tender. Transfer to a large bowl of iced water to cool, then drain well. Cut in half, removing the tough central vein, then dry the leaves on paper towel. Use about eight of the larger halves to line the greased bowl, overlapping them to completely cover the surface.

4 Melt the butter in a large saucepan over low heat, add the onion and garlic and cook for 5–6 minutes or until tender. Add the shredded cabbage and season with salt and pepper, then cover and cook for 5 minutes. Set aside to cool, then transfer to a bowl and combine with the prunes, bacon, sage, thyme, pork and allspice, and season well with salt and pepper.

5 Divide the mince stuffing into three even portions. Press the first portion over the base of the cabbage-lined bowl, then cover with about a third of the remaining halved cabbage leaves. Continue layering in this way until all the stuffing and cabbage leaves have been used. Bring any overlapping pieces of cabbage used to line the bowl up and over to cover the top. Cover the bowl tightly with foil then place in a large saucepan. Fill the saucepan with enough water to come a third of the way up the side of the bowl, and bring to the boil. Cover the saucepan with a tight-fitting lid, then reduce the heat and simmer for 45 minutes.

6 Once cooked, leave to cool for 10 minutes, then carefully remove the bowl from the pan. Turn out the stuffed cabbage onto a plate, cut into wedges and serve.

CONFIT DUCK AND LYCHEE SALAD

SERVES 6

This Asian-inspired dish is always popular. If you have a large enough mortar and pestle, you can grind the spices by hand. If not, an electric spice grinder is a great investment that you will use time and time again. The duck confit can be prepared in advance, and then reheated by removing the duck from the fat and baking for 20–25 minutes at 180°C before continuing with step 5.

1 cinnamon stick, broken
2 star anise, broken
2 teaspoons fennel seeds
50 g sea salt
4 duck marylands (leg and
   thigh portions)
1 kg duck fat
250 g green beans, tops trimmed

500 g lychees, peeled, seeded
   and halved
100 g bean sprouts
4 spring onions, trimmed and
   finely chopped
1 bunch coriander, leaves picked
1 bunch mint, leaves picked

DRESSING
1 small red chilli, sliced
100 g palm sugar, grated
100 ml lime juice
2 teaspoons fish sauce

1 To prepare the confit duck, place the cinnamon, star anise, fennel seeds and salt in a spice grinder and grind to a fine powder. Rub the spice powder over the marylands, then place them in a dish, cover with plastic film and marinate in the refrigerator for 6 hours.

2 Preheat the oven to 140°C.

3 Wash and dry the marylands well before placing them into a large heavy-based casserole with the duck fat. Place in the oven and cook for 4 hours or until the meat is very tender.

4 Remove the marylands from the fat and drain well (or if you're making this in advance, leave in the casserole to cool then cover and store in the fridge at this stage).

5 Spoon a tablespoon of duck fat from the casserole into a large frying pan and heat over medium–high heat. Add the marylands, skin-side down, reduce the heat to low–medium and cook for 10–15 minutes until the skin is golden and crispy. Leave to cool for 5 minutes, then carefully remove the meat from the bones and shred.

6 To make the dressing, place the chilli in a small saucepan along with the palm sugar and lime juice. Bring to the boil, then cook over low–medium heat for a couple of minutes, stirring until the palm sugar has completely dissolved. Stir in the fish sauce, then remove the pan from the heat and set aside.

7 Bring plenty of salted water to the boil in a large saucepan, add the green beans and blanch for 2–3 minutes, then refresh in iced water.

8 Place the beans in a bowl with the lychees, bean sprouts, spring onion, coriander and mint leaves, then toss gently to combine.

9 Mix the duck meat through the salad, then serve in individual bowls with the dressing alongside.

CELERIAC REMOULADE

SERVES 4

Remoulade is a dressing that is similar to mayonnaise, but is made with mustard. This dish is popular in France, and tastes especially good with grilled meat (like the dry-aged T-bone with bearnaise sauce on page 139), chicken or fish.

2½ tablespoons lemon juice
1 head celeriac, peeled and
   finely sliced

salt and pepper
2 egg yolks
1 tablespoon Dijon mustard

2 teaspoons seeded mustard
2 tablespoons white wine vinegar
200 ml vegetable oil

---

1 Half-fill a large bowl with cold water and stir in the lemon juice. Place four or five slices of celeriac on top of each other on a board, then slice into 2 mm strips and transfer to the bowl of water to prevent the celeriac from turning brown. Continue this process until all of the celeriac has been finely sliced. Add ½ teaspoon salt to the water and mix, then leave to stand for 10 minutes. Drain well, then gently squeeze the celeriac to remove as much excess water as possible.

2 To prepare the remoulade, whisk the egg yolks, mustards and vinegar until combined. Continue to whisk while pouring in the vegetable oil in a steady stream until thick and emulsified. Season with salt and pepper to taste. Whisk in a little water if the dressing is too thick.

3 Mix the shredded celeriac and the remoulade together until combined then season with salt and pepper to taste.

CAULIFLOWER PAKORAS

SERVES 4–6

These Indian-inspired treats are good as a side, but equally good to eat on their own. Serve them straight out of the oven.

---

vegetable oil, for deep-frying
⅔ cup (100 g) rice flour
⅔ cup (100 g) chickpea flour
2 teaspoons ground turmeric
2 teaspoons ground coriander
½ teaspoon chilli powder
2 teaspoons salt, plus extra to taste
2½ tablespoons lemon juice

1 cauliflower, cut into florets
½ red onion, finely chopped
30 g ginger, peeled and cut
    into thin strips
1 large red chilli, cut into
    thin strips
½ bunch coriander, leaves picked
    and roughly chopped

¾ bunch mint, leaves picked
    and roughly chopped
3 tablespoons Greek-style yoghurt
lime wedges and mango chutney,
    to serve

---

1 Preheat the oven to 100°C.

2 Heat the vegetable oil in a large heavy-based saucepan or deep-fryer to 170°C or until a cube of bread turns golden in 20 seconds.

3 Combine the flours, turmeric, ground coriander, chilli powder and salt in a bowl. Add the lemon juice and 150 ml water and whisk to form a smooth, thick batter.

4 In a separate bowl, toss together the cauliflower, onion, ginger, chilli, coriander and two-thirds of the mint until combined. Add this vegetable mixture to the batter and gently stir to combine.

5 Carefully place 4 or 5 heaped tablespoonfuls of the pakora mixture into the hot oil and cook for 2–3 minutes or until golden and crunchy – it's important to work in batches so you don't overcrowd the pan. Remove the pakoras with a slotted spoon and drain on paper towel, then lightly season with salt. Keep them warm in the oven while you make the rest.

6 Mix the yoghurt with the remaining chopped mint and transfer to a bowl.

7 Serve the pakoras hot with lime wedges, mango chutney and the minted yoghurt alongside for dipping.

ZUCCHINI WITH GARLIC, CHILLI AND LEMON

SERVES 6–8

The success of this tasty vegetable dish depends on using top-quality produce and not overcooking the zucchini and squash – they should be just lightly blanched. The garlic and chilli add some zing that complements the crispness of the vegetables.

---

4 zucchini (courgette) flowers,
    stems removed and reserved
5 yellow squash, cut into quarters
1 green zucchini (courgette),
    cut into wedges

1 yellow zucchini (courgette),
    cut into wedges
¼ cup (60 ml) olive oil
3 cloves garlic, sliced

1 large red chilli,
    finely sliced lengthways
salt and pepper
3 tablespoons finely grated parmesan
lemon juice, to taste

---

1 Blanch the zucchini flower stems, squash and zucchini in plenty of boiling salted water for 2 minutes, then drain.

2 Heat the oil in a large heavy-based frying pan over medium heat then add the garlic and cook, shaking the pan, for 2 minutes or until golden. Add the chilli, blanched stems, squash and zucchini and toss over medium heat for 2–3 minutes. Stir in the zucchini flowers, season with salt and pepper, and transfer to a large serving dish.

3 Top with the parmesan and squeeze over lemon juice to taste just before serving.

VEGETARIAN DINNER

SERVES 6

I find that more and more people are choosing vegetarian meals these days – for ideological or health reasons, or a combination of both. Here is my suggestion for a fresh, healthy and flavoursome starter and main – plus a wicked dessert, to tempt even the most virtuous.

A RELAXED DINNER, MEDITERRANEAN-STYLE

SERVES 4

You'll feel like you've been transported to Italy with this inspired menu. Serve the zucchini flowers and the artichokes together so your guests can graze for a while before you dish up the macaroni, then unveil the quince pie with a flourish. Make sure that you have plenty of fresh crusty bread and a good Italian red on hand.

LAMB FILLET SALAD WITH ROAST PUMPKIN AND PRESERVED LEMON

SERVES 4

The preserved lemon and harissa give this dish a lovely Moroccan flavour. Be careful not to overcook the lamb fillets as they don't have a high fat content to keep them moist.

---

100 ml olive oil
300 g butternut pumpkin (squash), peeled, seeded and cut into 2 cm cubes
8 lamb fillets, trimmed

salt and pepper
1 piece preserved lemon, rind only, rinsed and cut into fine strips
12 truss tomatoes, cut in half
¼ red onion, thinly sliced

¼ bunch mint, leaves picked and roughly chopped
juice of ½ lemon
1 teaspoon harissa
3 tablespoons Greek-style yoghurt

---

1 Preheat the oven to 180°C.

2 Heat half the oil in an ovenproof frying pan or flameproof casserole over high heat. Add the pumpkin and cook for about a minute or until golden, then turn the pumpkin pieces over and place the pan in the oven. Bake for 10–15 minutes or until tender. Remove and set aside to cool.

3 Heat a chargrill plate over high heat. Season the lamb fillets with salt and pepper and drizzle with a tablespoon of olive oil. Grill the lamb for 4 minutes, turning once, until cooked but still a little pink in the middle. Remove from the pan and leave to rest in a warm place.

4 Combine the preserved lemon, tomatoes, onion, mint and cooled roast pumpkin in a bowl. Season with salt and pepper and a few drops of lemon juice, then add the remaining olive oil and toss gently to combine.

5 Arrange the salad on individual plates or a serving platter. Cut each lamb fillet diagonally into six pieces and place on the salad. Mix together the harissa and yoghurt, spoon over the salad and serve.

BLUEFIN TUNA WITH CUCUMBER AND DAIKON SALAD

SERVES 6 AS A STARTER

At the restaurant I like to use a combination of belly and loin tuna for this salad (pictured overleaf) – it is worth making a visit to the sashimi stand at the fishmarkets or a specialty fishmonger to get these. If not, just buy the best-quality fresh tuna you can get your hands on. Enoki mushrooms, popular in Japanese cooking, have a delicate flavour that works well here. If you can't find any, substitute oyster mushrooms.

1 Lebanese (small) cucumber,
   thinly sliced
1 × 100 g piece daikon,
   thinly sliced
small handful coriander leaves
1 tablespoon pickled ginger
200 g enoki mushrooms,
   trimmed

600 g bluefin tuna fillet, bloodline
   removed, the thickest part cut into
   cubes, the rest thinly sliced

DRESSING
2 teaspoons sesame oil
3 tablespoons rice wine vinegar
3 tablespoons mirin
100 ml light soy sauce
2 teaspoons finely grated ginger
1 tablespoon finely grated daikon

1 To prepare the dressing, combine all the ingredients in a bowl and whisk to mix well. Stand for 20 minutes to allow the flavours to infuse, then strain the mixture through a sieve and set aside.

2 Mix the cucumber, daikon, coriander, pickled ginger and enoki mushrooms together in a bowl, then mix through a tablespoon of the dressing.

3 Place a mound of salad in the middle of each plate and arrange the tuna around this. Spoon over the remaining dressing and serve.

NASHI PEAR AND BLUE CHEESE SALAD

SERVES 4

Blue cheese and pears make a great classic combination. Pickled walnuts add an original twist – you should be able to find them at specialty grocers (I use English brand Opies).

1½ tablespoons sherry vinegar
75 ml olive oil
salt and pepper
1 head green witlof (chicory),
    leaves picked

1 head red witlof (chicory),
    leaves picked
½ head radicchio, leaves picked
½ bunch watercress
2 nashi pears, halved, cored and
    thinly sliced

100 g gorgonzola, cut into
    small chunks
2 tablespoons pine nuts, toasted
4 pickled walnuts, drained and
    thinly sliced

---

1 Whisk together the vinegar and olive oil until combined. Season with salt and pepper, then set aside until required.

2 Place the salad leaves and watercress in a large bowl. Add the pear slices, gorgonzola and pine nuts. Drizzle over the dressing and gently toss.

3 Arrange the salad onto four plates, top with pickled walnut slices and serve.

GLOBE ARTICHOKES WITH PARMESAN

SERVES 4

Many people are put off by the thought of preparing artichokes – but you shouldn't be. If you follow this recipe step by step, you will be rewarded with a uniquely flavoured dish you can serve as a starter or side dish.

⅓ cup (80 ml) olive oil
2 golden shallots, sliced
2 cloves garlic, crushed
1 bay leaf
2 sprigs thyme

1 teaspoon coriander seeds, crushed
salt and pepper
100 ml white wine
100 ml white wine vinegar
8 small or 4 large globe artichokes

1 lemon, cut in half
½ cup mesclun leaves
50 g parmesan, shaved
3 teaspoons balsamic glaze

1 Heat a tablespoon of the olive oil in a saucepan over medium heat, then add the shallot and garlic. Cook, stirring often, for 2–3 minutes or until softened. Add the bay leaf, thyme and coriander seeds, then season with salt and pepper. Pour in the wine, vinegar and 2 cups (500 ml) water, bring to the boil then reduce to a simmer.

2 Meanwhile, to prepare the artichokes, remove the tough outer leaves then, using a vegetable peeler, peel away the dark green layers to reveal the white hearts. Rub them immediately all over with the cut lemon to prevent them from browning.

3 Place the artichokes in the saucepan and cook in the simmering liquid for 10–15 minutes until tender. Remove the pan from the heat and allow the artichokes to cool in the liquid. Once cool, drain them well, then cut in half lengthways.

4 Heat 2 tablespoons of the olive oil over medium heat in a large, heavy-based frying pan, add the artichokes and fry for 2–3 minutes or until golden brown.

5 Arrange the artichokes on a serving platter, then scatter over the mesclun leaves and the shaved parmesan. Whisk the balsamic glaze with the remaining olive oil and drizzle over to finish.

DESSERTS

CHOCOLATE AND EARL GREY TEA TART

SERVES 8–10

If you are a chocolate-lover, it doesn't get much better than this. Just make sure you use the best-quality chocolate you can find. I use Valrhona Caraïbe dark chocolate, which is 66 per cent cocoa, or Valrhona Jivara milk chocolate, which is 40 per cent cocoa.

---

3 cups (750 ml) pouring cream
5 Earl Grey tea bags
50 g good-quality dark chocolate
420 g good-quality milk chocolate
50 g unsalted butter, softened
good-quality cocoa powder,
   for dusting

CHOCOLATE SPONGE
50 g good-quality dark chocolate
5 egg yolks
100 g caster sugar
1½ tablespoons good-quality
   cocoa powder
4 egg whites

CREME CHANTILLY
150 ml cream
1 tablespoon icing sugar
1 vanilla bean, seeds scraped and
   reserved, pod set aside for another
   use (you could use this to make
   vanilla-infused sugar, see page 8)

---

1 Firstly, make the chocolate sponge. Preheat the oven to 190°C and lightly grease a 30 cm × 40 cm baking tray, then line with non-stick baking paper.

2 Melt the 50 g dark chocolate in a dry heatproof bowl set over a saucepan of simmering water, making sure that you don't let any water come into contact with the chocolate. Once the chocolate has melted, transfer it to a mixing bowl and set aside to cool slightly.

3 In an electric mixer, whisk the egg yolks with half the caster sugar until thick and pale. Fold this into the melted chocolate, then fold in the cocoa.

4 Whisk the egg whites in the electric mixer until soft peaks form, then gradually add the remaining sugar and whisk until stiff peaks form. Gently fold this into the chocolate mixture until combined. Spread the mixture evenly onto the prepared tray to a thickness of 1 cm and top with another sheet of non-stick baking paper. Bake for about 10 minutes or until the sponge is just cooked and springy to the touch.

5 Meanwhile, bring the 3 cups (750 ml) cream to a simmer in a saucepan, then remove from the heat and add the tea bags, leaving to infuse while the cream cools to room temperature.

6 Lightly grease a 23 cm × 24 cm × 2.5 cm depth lamington or Swiss roll tin.

7 Remove the sponge from the oven and, when cool enough to handle, take a rolling pin and firmly roll it over the top sheet of non-stick baking paper. This will flatten the sponge and make it denser (you want it about 3 mm thick). Remove and discard the top layer of non-stick baking paper and then trim the sponge to fit the prepared tin. Pick up the ends of the bottom layer of non-stick baking paper and transfer the sponge to the tin – it should fit snugly. Fold the excess non-stick baking paper over the sides of the tin.

8 Melt the dark chocolate in a dry heatproof bowl set over a saucepan of simmering water, making sure that you don't let any water come into contact with the chocolate. Once melted, brush the chocolate evenly over the sponge and place the tin in the fridge for about 10 minutes to set.

9 Melt the milk chocolate in a dry heatproof bowl set over a saucepan of simmering water, making sure that you don't let any water come into contact with the chocolate. Once melted, pour the chocolate into the bowl of an electric mixer, then pour over the infused cream, discarding the tea bags. Mixing slowly, add the butter, a little at a time, and continue mixing until the chocolate cools, then pour this mixture evenly over the sponge and place the tin back in the fridge to set overnight.

10 To make the creme chantilly, place the cream, icing sugar and vanilla seeds into a large bowl and whip until firm.

11 Just prior to serving, remove the tart from the fridge, cut into rectangles about 6 cm × 9 cm and dust with a thick layer of cocoa powder. Serve with a generous dollop of creme chantilly.

WARM PEAR TART WITH CARAMEL SAUCE AND GINGER CRUMBLE

SERVES 6

Pears are available all year round, but are at their peak in autumn. Make sure you select pears that are just ripe, as if they are overripe they will not hold their shape when cooked. The Pernod adds a distinctive sweet-but-spicy flavour to this classic pear tart.

100 g marzipan, crumbled
1 egg white
¼ teaspoon vanilla extract
½ teaspoon plain flour
1 sheet puff pastry, thawed if frozen
2 beurre bosc pears, peeled, cored
　　and very thinly sliced
50 g unsalted butter, melted
255 g caster sugar
2 teaspoons Pernod
½ teaspoon fennel seeds

1½ tablespoons lemon juice
6 paradise pears, peeled
1 cup (250 ml) double cream,
　　lightly whipped

GINGER CRUMBLE
100 g butter
130 g plain flour
50 g caster sugar
1 teaspoon ground ginger

CARAMEL SAUCE
200 g caster sugar
100 g butter
200 ml cream

1 Preheat the oven to 200°C.

2 To make the caramel sauce, combine the caster sugar with 2½ tablespoons water in a small saucepan. Bring to the boil over low–medium heat, then increase the heat to medium–high and cook, shaking the pan now and then, for 3–4 minutes or until the sugar turns golden. Working quickly, remove the pan from the heat and, taking care as the mixture will spit, whisk in the butter until combined, then slowly pour in the cream and leave to cool to room temperature.

3 For the ginger crumble, place all the ingredients in a bowl and rub together with your fingers until the mixture resembles breadcrumbs. Scatter evenly onto a baking tray and bake for 5–6 minutes until golden brown, shaking the tray every now and again to ensure the crumble cooks evenly. Remove from the oven and set aside, leaving the oven set to 200°C.

4 Place the marzipan, egg white, vanilla extract and flour in a bowl and, using electric beaters, beat until smooth.

5 On a clean, lightly floured benchtop, roll the puff pastry sheet out to a 5 mm thickness and cut into a rectangle 16 cm × 22 cm. Place onto a baking tray lined with non-stick baking paper, and spread the marzipan mixture evenly over the pastry, leaving a 5 mm gap around the edge. Arrange the pear slices on the marzipan, overlapping them slightly, then brush over the melted butter and sprinkle over 55 g of the sugar. Transfer to the oven and bake for 20 minutes.

6 Meanwhile, in a large heavy-based saucepan, bring the remaining caster sugar, the Pernod, fennel seeds, lemon juice and 400 ml water to a boil. Place the whole pears in the syrup, reduce the heat to medium and simmer for about 10 minutes or until the pears are tender.

7 Remove the tart from the oven and spoon over half the caramel sauce. Place a sheet of non-stick baking paper on top of the tart and then place a baking tray face-down on top of that. Holding the trays firmly at each end, carefully invert the trays so the pastry base is uppermost, remove the top tray and layer of paper and return the tart to the oven for a further 10–15 minutes; this ensures the base is nice and crisp.

8 Remove the tart from the oven and carefully invert onto a serving tray. Drizzle over the remaining caramel sauce and arrange the whole poached pears on top. Sprinkle the crumble mix over, then serve with the whipped cream alongside.

PISTACHIO SOUFFLES

SERVES 4

Light as a feather, these souffles are easy to make and look glorious. Just note that they only hold their shape for a few minutes, so serve them straightaway. Pistachio paste is available at specialty grocers.

1 tablespoon cornflour
1 tablespoon pistachio paste
unsalted butter, softened, for brushing
50 g finely grated dark chocolate

5 egg whites
50 g caster sugar
icing sugar, for dusting

CHOCOLATE ICE CREAM
550 ml full-cream milk
1 cup (250 ml) skim milk
7 egg yolks
130 g caster sugar
225 g milk chocolate

1 Firstly, make the ice cream. Place the milks in a saucepan and bring to a simmer over medium heat.

2 In a bowl, whisk together the egg yolks and sugar, then pour a little of the simmering milk into the bowl and stir through. Once incorporated, transfer all the egg yolk mixture into the saucepan with the milk and cook over low heat, stirring constantly with a wooden spoon, for about 4–5 minutes or until the mixture coats the back of the spoon.

3 Strain through a fine-meshed sieve into a clean bowl then add the chocolate and stir until incorporated. Churn in an ice-cream machine according to the manufacturer's instructions, then cover and freeze until required.

4 To make the souffles, mix together the cornflour and 2 tablespoons water in a small mixing bowl.

5 Bring 85 ml water and the pistachio paste to the boil in a small saucepan, whisking to dissolve the paste. Add the cornflour mixture and cook, whisking continuously, over medium heat for 1 minute. Transfer to a mixing bowl, whisk until smooth and set aside to cool.

6 Preheat the oven to 190°C.

7 Using a pastry brush, brush the insides of four 120 ml souffle moulds with some softened butter. Place in the fridge to set for 5 minutes, then brush again with butter and coat with grated chocolate, tipping out any excess.

8 Whisk the egg whites in a large bowl until soft peaks form, then gradually add the sugar, whisking constantly, until stiff peaks form.

9 Using a spatula, gradually fold the egg white mixture into the cornflour mixture with a light touch, so as not to expel too much air. Divide the mixture among the prepared moulds, then place in the oven and cook for 4–5 minutes or until the souffles have risen 2–3 cm over the rim.

10 Dust the souffles with icing sugar and serve immediately, with some chocolate ice cream alongside.

STEAMED MANDARIN AND TREACLE PUDDINGS

SERVES 6

These are just the thing to finish off a long, lazy Sunday dinner. The sharp mandarin and sticky treacle are a perfect match. You can prepare these puddings in advance, store them in the fridge then pop them in the oven for 10–15 minutes to reheat them. Creme anglaise, a fancy name for custard, can be served warm or cold with any number of cakes and desserts. It adds a delightfully decadent touch to this dish.

175 g unsalted butter, softened, plus extra for greasing
½ cup (125 ml) treacle
175 g brown sugar
3 eggs
175 g self-raising flour, sifted

2 mandarins, peeled and segmented, pips removed
boiling water, to fill saucepan

CREME ANGLAISE
200 ml milk
200 ml cream
1 vanilla bean, split and seeds scraped
6 egg yolks
40 g caster sugar

1 Lightly grease six 200 ml metal pudding moulds with a little softened butter. Cut six circles of non-stick baking paper to fit neatly into the base of each mould and place these inside. Put half a tablespoon of treacle into each mould then set aside.

2 Cream the 175 g butter and sugar until light and fluffy. Add the eggs one at a time, beating well between each addition, then add the remaining treacle. Gently stir in the flour until combined. Place a spoonful of this mixture into each of the moulds, then place two segments of mandarin on top. Continue this process of layering the mixture and all except six of the mandarin segments until the moulds are three-quarters full, finishing with a layer of mixture, then cover each mould with a small piece of buttered foil.

3 Place the moulds in a large saucepan. Fill with boiling water to come halfway up the sides of the moulds, then cover and simmer over medium heat for 40 minutes or until cooked through when tested with a skewer.

4 Meanwhile, to make the creme anglaise, place the milk, cream and vanilla seeds in a saucepan and bring to a simmer over medium heat.

5 In a bowl, whisk together the egg yolks and sugar, then pour a little of the simmering milk mixture into the bowl and stir through. Once incorporated, transfer all the egg yolk mixture into the saucepan with the milk mixture and cook over low heat, stirring constantly with a wooden spoon, for about 4–5 minutes or until the mixture coats the back of the spoon, then strain.

6 Carefully remove the moulds from the pan, take off the foil and run a knife around the inside of each mould and turn the puddings out into a serving dish.

7 Pour the creme anglaise into the base of the dish, top each pudding with a mandarin segment and serve immediately.

MANGO CHEESECAKE WITH COCONUT SAGO

SERVES 8

This great take on the classic cheesecake is the perfect end to a summer's dinner. Start the cheesecakes the day before so that they have time to set properly, and make sure you use gold-strength gelatine leaves. They are fairly simple to unmould by hand – if you are having trouble, just rub the outside of the moulds with your fingers to generate some heat and the cake should slide out.

3 mangoes, peeled and stones removed, 2 roughly chopped, 1 cubed
4 leaves gold-strength gelatine
500 g cream cheese, softened
80 g caster sugar
1 tablespoon lime juice
small handful baby coriander or regular coriander, to garnish

COCONUT SAGO
¼ cup (50 g) sago
400 ml milk
1½ tablespoons caster sugar
200 ml coconut cream

GINGER CRUMBLE
100 g ginger nut biscuits, coarsely crumbled
50 g Granita biscuits, coarsely crumbled
1½ tablespoons butter, melted

1 For the cheesecake filling, place the roughly chopped mango flesh in a food processor or blender and process to a smooth puree. Remove half the puree, transfer to a jug and set aside to use later.

2 Meanwhile, soften the gelatine in cold water for a minute or so, then remove and place in a saucepan over very low heat until melted.

3 Add the cream cheese and sugar to the remaining puree in the food processor and process until the mixture is very smooth and the sugar has dissolved. With the motor running, add the melted gelatine and the lime juice and process until smooth. Divide the mixture among eight 8 cm diameter aluminium ring moulds, then refrigerate overnight or until set.

4 To make the coconut sago, soak the sago in enough water to cover for 1 hour, then place in a sieve, rinse under cold running water and drain well.

5 Place the sago, milk and sugar in a saucepan and simmer over low heat, stirring often, for 20 minutes or until the sago is translucent. Allow to cool, then stir in the coconut cream and refrigerate until required.

6 Preheat the oven to 180°C.

7 Place the crumbled biscuits into a food processor and blend to fine crumbs. Transfer to a large bowl and mix in the melted butter, then spread the mixture out onto a baking tray, pressing down to form a thin layer. Bake for 6–7 minutes or until golden, then remove from the oven and allow to cool slightly.

8 Working quickly, take the ring moulds from the fridge and carefully press each one into the crumb mixture, then sprinkle some more mixture on top and press down lightly. To unmould, hold the ring over a serving plate and push lightly on top – the warmth of your fingers will loosen the cheesecake and it should slide out.

9 Serve the cheesecakes along with a couple of spoonfuls of sago, some reserved mango puree, mango cubes and coriander.

STRAWBERRY SHORTCAKE

SERVES 4

An oldie but a goodie, this is wonderful with a glass of dessert wine. Be very careful when you remove the fragile shortbread from the tray and spread it with the mascarpone mixture.

---

200 g plain flour
pinch of salt
40 g rice flour
175 g cold unsalted butter, chopped

90 g caster sugar, plus
2 teaspoons extra
½ cup (125 g) mascarpone
⅓ cup (55 g) icing sugar

1 vanilla bean, split and seeds scraped
400 g strawberries, hulled and halved
3 teaspoons orange blossom water
6 mint leaves, finely sliced

---

1 Preheat the oven to 160°C and grease and line a 30 cm x 20 cm baking tray.

2 Sieve the plain flour, salt and rice flour into a bowl. Grate the cold butter onto the flour mixture, then add the 90 g caster sugar and rub together using the palms of your hands until the mixture resembles fine breadcrumbs.

3 Spread the mixture over the prepared tray and lightly press down to form an even layer about 1 cm thick. Bake for 20 minutes or until light golden.

4 Remove the tray from the oven, sprinkle the remaining caster sugar over the shortbread then leave to cool.

5 To prepare the filling, place the mascarpone, 3 tablespoons of the icing sugar and the vanilla seeds in a bowl and mix together, then set aside until required.

6 Place the strawberries in a bowl with the orange blossom water, mint and remaining icing sugar and toss to combine. Leave to infuse for 5 minutes.

7 Carefully remove the cooled shortbread from the tray and transfer to a large serving board. Top with some of the mascarpone mixture and the macerated strawberries, then serve with the remaining mascarpone mixture alongside for guests to dollop on top.

BANANA AND PASSIONFRUIT SORBET

SERVES 6

Just the thing to serve at the end of a filling meal. Take it out of the freezer a few minutes before you wish to serve it, so that it is not too cold.

⅓ cup (75 g) caster sugar
8 passionfruit, pulp removed
3 ripe bananas, peeled
juice of 1 lime

1 Place the sugar and 75 ml water in a saucepan and bring to a simmer, stirring constantly over a low heat to dissolve the sugar. Remove from the heat and set aside to cool.

2 Push the passionfruit pulp through a fine-meshed sieve, extracting as much juice as possible. Reserve 1 tablespoon of seeds from the sieve, then discard the remainder.

3 Place the bananas, passionfruit juice and lime juice in a food processor or blender and process to a smooth puree.

4 Transfer to a bowl, then stir in the cooled sugar syrup and reserved passionfruit seeds. Refrigerate the mixture until chilled, then churn in an ice-cream machine according to the manufacturer's instructions. Freeze until required.

RASPBERRY RIPPLE ICE CREAM

SERVES 6

The best time to buy fresh raspberries is in summer or early autumn, when they are in season. This ice cream is delicious served with fresh raspberries and a glass of dessert wine.

½ vanilla bean, split and seeds scraped
2 cups (500 ml) milk
10 egg yolks
100 g caster sugar
½ cup (125 ml) pouring cream
300 g raspberries

1 Place the vanilla seeds, milk, egg yolks and sugar in a bowl and whisk to combine well, then transfer to a saucepan and cook over low heat, stirring constantly with a wooden spoon, for about 4–5 minutes or until the mixture coats the back of the spoon.

2 Strain through a fine-meshed sieve into a clean bowl, place a piece of plastic film directly on the surface of the custard to prevent a skin forming and leave to cool to room temperature. Refrigerate for about 1 hour or until chilled.

3 Meanwhile, place the raspberries in a blender and process until smooth, then strain into a saucepan. Cook over medium–high heat for 6–7 minutes or until reduced and thickened to a syrup consistency. Cool to room temperature, then place in the fridge to chill.

4 Stir the cream through the chilled custard mixture, then churn in an ice-cream machine according to the manufacturer's instructions. Transfer to a large bowl, add the chilled raspberry syrup and lightly stir in to achieve a ripple effect. Freeze until firm, then serve.

PLUM AND ALMOND TART

SERVES 8

A truly autumnal dessert, best served warm with a dollop of cream or vanilla ice cream (see page 212).
Start making the dough well in advance, to allow enough time to refrigerate it before baking.

---

100 g unsalted butter, chopped
3 large egg whites
⅓ cup (40 g) ground almonds
100 g icing sugar,
   plus extra for dusting

35 g honey
40 g plain flour
8–12 plums, cut in half,
   stones removed and sliced

PASTRY
325 g flour
pinch of salt
175 g cold butter, chopped
90 g icing sugar
1 egg

---

1 To make the pastry, combine the flour, salt, butter and icing sugar in a food processor and process until the mixture resembles fine breadcrumbs. Beat in the egg then turn the mixture out onto a lightly floured benchtop and knead until the dough just comes together. Form the dough into a disc, cover with plastic film and refrigerate for 2–3 hours.

2 Roll out the chilled pastry until large enough to cover the base and sides of a 28 cm tart tin with a removable base, then line the tin with the pastry and trim the sides. Refrigerate for 1 hour.

3 Preheat the oven to 180°C.

4 Line the pastry case with non-stick baking paper and fill with baking beads or dried beans. Blind bake for 15–20 minutes or until golden, then remove the paper and beans and set the tart case aside.

5 Meanwhile, melt the butter in a frying pan over medium heat then cook for 3–4 minutes or until nut-brown. Remove from the heat and leave to cool.

6 In a bowl, whisk together the egg whites, ground almonds, icing sugar, honey and flour until the mixture is smooth, then stir in the butter. Pour the mixture into the still-warm tart case then arrange the plum slices evenly over.

7 Bake for 30 minutes or until the pastry is golden and the almond mixture is firm.

8 Serve warm or at room temperature, lightly dusted with icing sugar.

PEACH TART WITH CARAMEL SAUCE

SERVES 6

A simple but delicious dessert. This is how the classic French dessert, tarte tatin, used to be made, before people started to cook it in a pan. You could just as easily use apples or pears for a bit of variety.

3 sheets puff pastry,
  thawed if frozen
3 large yellow freestone peaches,
  halved, stones removed,
  cut into 2 mm slices

100 g unsalted butter, melted
100 g caster sugar
1 tablespoon icing sugar
200 g mascarpone

CARAMEL SAUCE
150 g caster sugar
150 ml pouring cream
75 g unsalted butter

1 For the caramel sauce, combine the sugar with 2½ tablespoons water in a small saucepan. Bring slowly to the boil, then cook over medium–high heat for 3–4 minutes or until a dark caramel forms. Remove from the heat, then quickly add the cream and butter – take care as the mixture will spit. Whisk until smooth and well combined, then leave to cool to room temperature.

2 Preheat the oven to 180°C and line two baking trays with non-stick baking paper.

3 Cut out two 13 cm rounds from each sheet of puff pastry and place on the prepared baking trays. Arrange the peach slices over the pastry rounds in a spiral shape, overlapping them slightly, then brush with melted butter and sprinkle with caster sugar. Bake for 20 minutes or until the pastry is puffed and golden.

4 Remove the tarts from the oven and spread with some of the caramel sauce, then carefully turn them upside-down and place them back on the trays. Return to the oven and bake for a further 10 minutes or until caramelised.

5 To serve, spoon some of the caramel sauce onto the plate and drag the spoon through it. Place a tart alongside, peach-side up. Mix together the icing sugar and mascarpone and, using a hot spoon, place a smooth dollop of this mixture onto each plate and serve.

PUMPKIN AND LIME CHEESECAKE

SERVES 8

A new twist on an old favourite. When you're making the jelly, be sure to use gold-strength gelatine or the jelly will not set properly.

---

40 g unsalted butter
500 g butternut pumpkin,
   peeled, seeded and chopped
300 g cream cheese
100 g mascarpone
1 egg
4 egg yolks
100 g caster sugar
1 vanilla bean, split and seeds scraped

GINGERBREAD BASE
300 g ginger nut biscuits, broken
90 g unsalted butter, melted,
   plus extra for greasing

LIME JELLY
40 g sugar
1 cup (250 ml) lime juice
   (from about 8 limes)
3 leaves gold-strength gelatine

---

1 Preheat the oven to 160°C. Line the base of a 19 cm springform cake tin with non-stick baking paper, then lightly grease the sides.

2 To make the gingerbread base, place the biscuits in a food processor and process to fine crumbs, then add the butter and process until well combined. Transfer the biscuit mixture to the prepared tin, pressing it down firmly into the base and the sides to make sure there are no gaps. Transfer to the oven and bake for 10–15 minutes, then remove and set aside to cool. Reduce the oven temperature to 110°C.

3 Melt the butter in a saucepan over low–medium heat. Add the pumpkin, cover then cook, stirring occasionally, for 20 minutes or until the pumpkin is very tender. Remove the lid then cook, stirring, for another 5 minutes or until any excess liquid has evaporated. Cool the mixture, then transfer to a blender or food processor and process to a smooth puree.

4 Combine the cream cheese, mascarpone, egg and egg yolks, sugar and vanilla seeds in a food processor then process until the mixture is smooth. Transfer to a bowl and stir in the pumpkin puree until well combined. Pour this mixture onto the cooled gingerbread base, then bake in the oven for 40 minutes; the cheesecake should still be slightly wobbly in the centre. Leave to cool to room temperature, then refrigerate for 1 hour or until set.

5 Meanwhile, to make the lime jelly, first make a sugar syrup. Place the sugar and 40 ml water into a small saucepan over low heat and stir until the sugar has dissolved. Remove from the heat and allow to cool. Add the lime juice to the pan and bring to a simmer, then remove from the heat.

6 Soften the gelatine in a bowl of cold water, then squeeze out the excess water and add the softened gelatine to the warm lime liquid. Stir well to dissolve the gelatine, then set aside for about 10 minutes to cool to room temperature (take care not to leave it too long as the mixture will start to set).

7 Pour the lime jelly over the top of the chilled cheesecake and leave to set in the fridge for 30 minutes before serving.

QUINCE TART

SERVES 12

There is nothing quite like the gentle aroma of quinces poaching. As they cook, they turn from a pale yellow-white to a rich ruby-red, and the taste is sublime. For this recipe, you can poach the quinces a day or so in advance and store them in the fridge until you're ready to make the tart.

200 ml red wine
150 g caster sugar
1 cinnamon stick
zest of 1 lemon, all white pith removed
2 quinces, peeled, cored and cut into
   8 wedges

150 g unsalted butter
150 g icing sugar
3 eggs
150 g ground almonds
whipped cream, to serve

PASTRY
180 g cold unsalted butter, chopped
2 cups (300 g) plain flour
90 g icing sugar, sifted
1 egg
1 egg yolk, beaten

1 Preheat the oven to 160°C.

2 To make the pastry, place the butter, flour and icing sugar in a bowl and, using your fingertips, rub the butter in until the mixture resembles coarse breadcrumbs. Add the whole egg then mix together using a flat-bladed knife until a dough forms. Form the pastry into a disc, wrap in plastic film and refrigerate for 2 hours.

3 On a lightly floured benchtop, roll out the pastry to a 5 mm thickness, then carefully place it into a 27 cm tart tin with a removable base, easing it into the sides. Trim the edges, then line with non-stick baking paper and fill with baking beads or dried beans. Blind bake for 15 minutes, then remove from the oven.

4 Remove the baking paper and beans and brush the tart case with a thin coating of egg yolk to seal, then return to the oven to cook for a further 5 minutes. Remove from the oven and set aside until required. Increase the oven temperature to 180°C.

5 Meanwhile, place the red wine, sugar, cinnamon stick and lemon zest in a saucepan and bring to a simmer. Add the quince wedges and pour in enough cold water to just cover them. Bring to a simmer, then cook over low heat for 20 minutes or until tender. Remove the quince wedges with a slotted spoon and set aside, reserving 1 cup (250 ml) of the cooking liquid.

6 Cream the butter and icing sugar using hand-held electric beaters until light and fluffy. Add the eggs one at a time, beating well after each addition. Stir in the ground almonds, then pour this mixture into the tart case, smoothing it evenly to the edges. Arrange the poached quince wedges on top and bake the tart for 25 minutes or until it is light golden.

7 While the tart is baking, boil the reserved cooking liquid over high heat for 5–8 minutes or until it is reduced and a thick syrup has formed. Brush a little of this syrup over the tart when it comes out of the oven. Leave the tart to cool for at least 20 minutes before slicing and serving with a dollop of whipped cream.

CHOCOLATE FONDANTS WITH RASPBERRIES AND VANILLA ICE CREAM

SERVES 6

A classic combination that never fails to delight. You can make the chocolate fondants well ahead of time and store them in the fridge, then pop them into a preheated oven as your guests are finishing off their main course. I like to use Valrhona Grand Cru Manjari chocolate, which has 64 per cent cocoa, and produces a lovely light cake with a gooey, oozy chocolate centre. I often make one extra to 'sacrifice', cutting it open to make sure the fondant has reached the right consistency.

---

softened butter, for greasing
cocoa, for sprinkling
300 g unsalted butter
300 g good-quality dark chocolate
6 eggs
6 egg yolks
30 g plain flour, sieved
160 g caster sugar

150 g raspberries
1½ tablespoons finely sliced
   mint leaves

RASPBERRY COULIS
250 g raspberries
¼ cup (40 g) icing sugar

VANILLA ICE CREAM
2 cups (500 ml) milk
½ vanilla bean, split and
   seeds scraped
½ cup (110 g) caster sugar
12 egg yolks
1 cup (250 ml) pouring cream

---

1 To make the ice cream, combine the milk, vanilla seeds and pod in a saucepan and bring almost to the boil, then remove from the heat.

2 In a bowl, whisk together the sugar and egg yolks then add to the warm milk mixture and return the pan to the stove over a low–medium heat. Stirring constantly with a wooden spoon, cook for 4–5 minutes or until the mixture thickens enough to coat the back of the spoon. Strain, discarding the solids, then leave to cool to room temperature, stirring often to prevent a skin forming. Stir in the cream then refrigerate until chilled. Churn in an ice-cream machine according to the manufacturer's instructions, then cover and freeze until required.

3 Grease six 150 ml dariole or pudding moulds with the softened butter, making sure the base and sides are thoroughly coated. Sprinkle over the cocoa, shaking out any excess. Place the prepared moulds in the refrigerator to chill until ready to use.

4 Place the unsalted butter and chocolate in a dry heatproof bowl set over a saucepan of simmering water, making sure that you don't let any water come into contact with the chocolate. Without stirring, leave the

mixture over medium heat until melted. Once melted, remove the bowl from the heat and gently stir in the eggs and yolks until combined, trying to incorporate as little air as possible. Stir in the flour and caster sugar and pour the mixture into the prepared moulds until two-thirds full. Tap the base of the moulds on the bench to expel any air. Refrigerate for a minimum of 5 hours, or preferably overnight if you have the time.

5 Preheat the oven to 175°C.

6 For the coulis, combine the raspberries and icing sugar in a food processor and process for 1 minute or until smooth. Strain the mixture through a fine-meshed sieve to remove the seeds, then refrigerate until required.

7 Transfer the moulds from the fridge to the preheated oven and bake for 9 minutes.

8 Place the fresh raspberries in a bowl with the mint and stir through the coulis.

9 Gently invert the moulds to turn out and serve warm with ice cream and some raspberries in coulis.

PEDRO XIMENEZ ICE CREAM WITH ORANGE AND RAISINS

SERVES 6

Pedro Ximenez is a sweet sherry from Spain, with a smooth consistency and a treacly, raisin-like flavour, that is now widely available from good bottle shops. Do not skimp on the quality of the sherry or the ice cream will suffer. The macerated raisins need to be soaked overnight, so start this dish the day before you wish to serve it. For this recipe, you'll need six moulds, each 2.5 cm deep and 7 cm in diameter (these are available from kitchen supply stores).

---

icing sugar, to dust
2 navel oranges, peeled and segmented

MACERATED RAISINS
2 tablespoons Pedro Ximenez
  (or other good-quality sweet sherry)
35 g caster sugar
100 g raisins

ALMOND SPONGE
5 egg whites
205 g caster sugar
155 g ground almonds

PEDRO XIMENEZ ICE CREAM
10 egg yolks
150 g caster sugar
75 ml Pedro Ximenez (or other
  good-quality sweet sherry)
850 ml pouring cream

CANDIED ORANGE ZEST
75 g caster sugar
2 Valencia oranges, zest removed
  in strips with a vegetable peeler
¼ cup (60 ml) grenadine

---

1 To prepare the raisins, heat the sherry, sugar and 1½ tablespoons water in a small saucepan. Bring to the boil, add the raisins and remove the pan from the heat. Leave overnight to macerate.

2 For the almond sponge, preheat the oven to 220°C and line two baking trays with non-stick baking paper.

3 Using electric beaters, whisk together the egg whites until soft peaks form. Whisking constantly, slowly add half the sugar until the mixture is firm and glossy. Combine the ground almonds and remaining sugar in a bowl, then fold this mixture into the whipped whites.

4 Divide the mixture between the trays, spreading out into even layers about 1 cm thick, then bake for 5 minutes or until a light golden brown. Leave to cool then cut out twelve rounds using a 7 cm diameter biscuit cutter.

5 To make the ice cream, whisk together the egg yolks and sugar in a bowl until thick and pale. Add the sherry, whisk well to combine, then add the cream and whisk again to combine. Churn in an ice-cream machine according to the manufacturer's instructions, then spoon into six 7 cm diameter moulds and freeze until required.

6 To prepare the candied orange zest, first make a sugar syrup. Place the sugar and 75 ml water into a small saucepan over low heat and stir until the sugar has dissolved. Remove from the heat and allow to cool.

7 Blanch the orange zest in a saucepan of boiling water for 1–2 minutes. Remove and refresh in a bowl of iced water, then transfer to the saucepan with the sugar syrup and add the grenadine.

8 Return this to the stove and bring to the boil, reduce the heat to low and cook for 10–15 minutes until tender. Leave to cool before serving.

9 Drain off any excess liquid from the soaked raisins.

10 To serve, place a disc of almond sponge on a plate, then take a mould and place it over the disc, warming the outside with your hands so that the ice cream slides out onto the sponge. Top with another disc of sponge then dust with icing sugar. Arrange the orange segments, soaked raisins and some candied zest around the ice cream and serve.

GRILLED PINEAPPLE WITH CHILLI SYRUP

SERVES 6

I love to serve this dessert in summer: it's so quick and easy and it tastes fantastic. The chilli syrup really enhances the fresh flavour of the grilled pineapple. Use Bethonga Gold pineapples if you can get them: their intense sweetness really makes this dish.

100 g caster sugar
2 small red chillies, cut into thin strips,
    seeds removed
1 large ripe pineapple, peeled and
    cored, 'eyes' removed, cut into
    6 even slices
vanilla ice cream (see page 212),
    to serve

1 Combine the caster sugar and 100 ml water in a small saucepan and stir over medium heat until the sugar has dissolved. Place the chilli in the pan and bring to a simmer, cooking for 5 minutes before removing the pan from the heat and setting aside to cool.

2 Preheat a grill to high and grill the pineapple slices for 3–4 minutes on each side.

3 Place a grilled pineapple slice in the centre of each plate then scoop some vanilla ice cream on top. Drizzle over the cooled syrup and serve.

PEACH SOUFFLES WITH LEMONGRASS-INFUSED PEACHES

SERVES 4

A high-impact dessert with a lovely, delicate flavour. Don't be put off by the prospect of making a souffle –
it is really pretty straightforward. The lemongrass adds a pleasing hint of citrus.

---

1 large ripe peach
unsalted butter, for greasing
50 g caster sugar, plus extra for dusting

2 tablespoons cornflour
3 teaspoons lemon juice
4 egg whites

LEMONGRASS-INFUSED PEACHES
1½ cups (375 ml) white wine
100 g caster sugar
1 stick lemongrass, bruised
2 large ripe peaches

---

1 To make the lemongrass-infused peaches, place the wine, sugar and ½ cup (125 ml) water in a saucepan. Tie the lemongrass stick in a knot, then add to the pan. Bring the mixture to a simmer over low heat, stirring constantly to dissolve the sugar, then cover and keep warm.

2 Meanwhile, bring a saucepan of water to the boil. Using a small, sharp knife, make a small cross in the base of all three peaches then add them to the boiling water and blanch for 1 minute. Using a slotted spoon, carefully remove the peaches, then plunge into a bowl of iced water. Drain well, then peel off the skins, reserving one whole peach to use later.

3 Cut the other two peaches in half, then remove the stones and cut each half into quarters. Add to the lemongrass syrup, then return the syrup to a simmer. Cook the peaches over low heat for 2–3 minutes or until just softened. Remove from the heat, discarding the lemongrass.

4 Preheat the oven to 180°C.

5 Grease six 120 ml capacity souffle moulds with butter, dust lightly with caster sugar, then place in the freezer for about 10 minutes to firm the butter. Grease, dust and freeze again for 10 minutes.

6 Chop the flesh of the reserved peach and transfer to a food processor or blender, then process to a smooth puree. Measure out 150 ml of the puree (reserving any leftover for another use), place in a small saucepan and bring to a simmer over low heat.

7 Meanwhile, mix the cornflour and lemon juice in a small bowl, stirring until smooth, then whisk into the hot peach puree in the saucepan. Cook, whisking constantly, for 1 minute or until boiled and thickened. Remove from the heat and set aside to cool.

8 Place the egg whites in a large, clean, dry mixing bowl and whisk until soft peaks form, then slowly add the 50 g sugar, continuing to whisk, until firm peaks form; the mixture should be firm and glossy. Fold half of the whisked egg whites into the peach puree mixture, then gently fold in the remaining half.

9 Carefully divide the mixture among the prepared souffle moulds then bake for 8–10 minutes or until the souffles have risen 2–3 cm over the rim.

10 Serve each souffle with two quarters of lemongrass-infused peach and some syrup spooned over.

FIG KOUING-AMAN WITH RASPBERRY COULIS

SERVES 6

Kouing-aman (pictured overleaf) is a buttery pastry, similar to a croissant but much sweeter, which originated in Brittany in France. Its name means 'butter cake' in the Breton dialect, and it has a cult following – so much so that it has its own Facebook page! Its appearance doesn't have to be perfect – it is meant to look a bit rustic. Instead of figs, you could try wedges of peeled apple or pear. You could also serve it with vanilla ice cream (see page 212).

120 g plain flour
pinch of salt
½ teaspoon instant dried yeast
110 g butter, softened,
    plus extra for greasing
6 fresh figs

100 g caster sugar,
    plus extra for sprinkling
fresh fig quarters and
    fresh berries, to serve
icing sugar, for dusting

RASPBERRY COULIS
375 g raspberries
2½ tablespoons icing sugar

1 Combine the flour, salt and yeast in a bowl, then rub in 2 teaspoons of the softened butter with your fingers until the mixture resembles fine breadcrumbs. Add 75 ml tepid water and stir to make a soft dough. Place in a lightly greased bowl, cover with plastic film and set aside for 30 minutes at room temperature.

2 Transfer the dough to a lightly floured benchtop and roll out into a 20 cm x 30 cm rectangle about 5–6 mm thick.

3 Thinly slice the remaining butter and distribute the slices evenly over two-thirds of the dough, leaving a 5 mm border around the edge.

4 Fold the uncovered third of the dough over to cover the middle third, then fold the last third over to form a neat rectangle. Gently press the edges to seal. Wrap in plastic film and refrigerate for 30 minutes, then roll out again to a 20 cm x 30 cm rectangle. Sprinkle the 100 g caster sugar over two-thirds of the dough and repeat the folding process. Wrap in plastic film and refrigerate again for 30 minutes.

5 Preheat the oven to 180°C and grease six holes of a jumbo muffin tray with butter.

6 Roll the dough out again to a 20 cm x 30 cm rectangle then cut into six 10 cm squares. Place a fig in the centre of each square then bring the corners of the square up around the fig to enclose, gently pushing the ends together to seal. Place some extra caster sugar in a bowl and dip the pastries in the sugar to coat, then place in the muffin tray. Bake for 25 minutes or until golden.

7 Meanwhile, make the raspberry coulis. Blend the raspberries and icing sugar until smooth, then strain, discarding the seeds.

8 Place the warm pastries on a large platter with the fresh figs and berries, and lightly dust with icing sugar. Serve the raspberry coulis alongside.

STOCKS AND SAUCES

A homemade stock can make all the difference to your cooking, adding depth of flavour and character to even the simplest dish. And don't be afraid of using sauces to complete a dish – they are simpler than you might think and add that special finishing touch to a meal. Included here are my favourite stock recipes and a couple of sauces that you can easily master. Most of these can be made in advance and stored in the fridge or freezer, to take a bit of the pressure off when you next entertain.

CHICKEN STOCK

MAKES 2 LITRES

2.5 kg chicken bones or wings
1 onion, roughly chopped
3 stalks celery, roughly chopped
2 leeks, well washed and roughly chopped
1 bulb garlic, cut in half crossways
1 bunch thyme
2 bay leaves
10 white peppercorns

1 Place the chicken bones or wings in a large saucepan or stockpot and cover with water. Bring to a simmer and skim off any impurities. Reduce the heat to low and add the onion, celery, leek, garlic, thyme, bay leaves and peppercorns. Simmer for 4 hours, skimming occasionally.

2 Strain through a fine-meshed sieve, leave to cool and use as required.

VEGETABLE STOCK

MAKES ABOUT 3 LITRES

100 g butter
3 carrots, finely chopped
2 brown onions, finely chopped
1 leek, well washed and finely chopped
1 small bulb fennel, finely chopped
1 head celery, finely chopped
salt and pepper
3 cloves garlic, chopped
1 sprig tarragon
1 sprig thyme
1 bay leaf
1 tablespoon coriander seeds, crushed
300 ml white wine
½ bunch basil
½ bunch flat-leaf parsley
½ bunch chervil

1 Place the butter in a large saucepan or stockpot with all of the vegetables, season lightly and cook for 3–4 minutes over medium heat or until the onions are translucent. Add the garlic, tarragon, thyme, bay leaf, crushed coriander seeds and white wine and cook for 2 minutes.

2 Pour in about 4 litres water, bring to a simmer and cook for 10 minutes over medium heat, then season to taste.

3 Remove from the heat and add the basil, parsley and chervil, then set aside for 15 minutes before straining through a fine-meshed sieve. Leave to cool and use as required.

Stocks can be made ahead of time and stored in the fridge for up to 4 days or in the freezer for several weeks.

FISH STOCK

MAKES 2.5 LITRES

vegetable oil, for cooking
2 onions, chopped
1 leek, well washed and chopped
2 stalks celery, chopped
1 bulb fennel, chopped
6 cloves garlic
2.5 kg cod or snapper bones, roughly chopped
    and rinsed well
200 ml dry vermouth (I like to use Noilly Prat)
200 ml white wine
1 teaspoon white peppercorns
1 bay leaf
2 sprigs thyme
1 bunch flat-leaf parsley

1 Heat the oil in a large stockpot, add the onion, leek, celery, fennel and garlic and cook over medium heat for 4–5 minutes until softened but not coloured.

2 Add the chopped fish bones, vermouth and white wine and cook for 5 minutes. Pour in 2.5 litres water and bring to a simmer, skimming off any scum that forms on the surface. Add the remaining ingredients and simmer for 20 minutes.

3 Strain through a fine-meshed sieve, leave to cool and use as required.

VEAL STOCK

MAKES 3–4 LITRES

3 kg veal bones
1 tablespoon vegetable oil
1 onion, chopped
½ bulb garlic, cut crossways
1 leek, white part only, well washed and chopped
1 stalk celery, chopped
1 carrot, chopped
2 bay leaves
½ bunch thyme
1 teaspoon white peppercorns
300 ml red wine

1 Preheat the oven to 160°C.

2 Place the veal bones in a roasting tin and roast for about 50 minutes or until golden brown.

3 Heat the oil in a large saucepan or stockpot, add the onion, garlic, leek, celery, carrot, bay leaves, thyme and peppercorns and cook over medium heat for 10–15 minutes or until the vegetables have softened and the onions are golden brown.

4 Deglaze with the red wine, scraping all the sediment from the bottom of the pan, then add the roasted veal bones and cover with 5 litres cold water. Bring to a simmer, then reduce the heat to low and simmer gently for 4–5 hours, regularly skimming any scum that rises to the surface.

5 Strain the stock through a fine-meshed sieve, leave to cool and use as required.

CHICKEN JUS

MAKES ABOUT 1 LITRE

50 ml vegetable oil
1 kg chicken wings, roughly chopped
  (ask your butcher to do this for you)
1 carrot, diced
1 onion, diced
¼ stalk celery, chopped
200 ml white wine
1.5 litres chicken stock (see page 222)
2 cloves garlic, chopped
2 sprigs thyme

1 Heat the vegetable oil in a large saucepan or stockpot, add the chopped chicken wings and cook over high heat until golden brown, stirring occasionally. Pour off any excess fat then add the carrot, onion and celery and cook for 2–3 minutes. Add the white wine and simmer until the liquid is reduced by half.

2 Add all the other ingredients, reduce the heat to medium and simmer for 45–50 minutes, skimming occasionally.

3 Strain the stock through a fine-meshed sieve placed over a clean saucepan, discarding the solids. Simmer over medium heat until reduced to a sauce consistency. Strain again, leave to cool and use as required.

VEAL JUS

MAKES ABOUT 1 LITRE

3 kg veal bones
1 tablespoon vegetable oil
1 onion, chopped
½ bulb garlic, cut crossways
1 leek, white part only, well washed and chopped
1 stalk celery, chopped
1 carrot, chopped
2 bay leaves
½ bunch thyme
1 teaspoon white peppercorns
300 ml red wine

1 Preheat the oven to 160°C.

2 Place the veal bones in a roasting tin and roast for about 50 minutes or until golden brown.

3 Heat the oil in a large saucepan or stockpot, add the onion, garlic, leek, celery, carrot, bay leaves, thyme and peppercorns and cook over medium heat for 10–15 minutes or until the vegetables have softened and the onions are golden brown.

4 Deglaze the pan with the red wine, scraping all the sediment from the bottom of the pan, then add the roasted veal bones and cover with 5 litres cold water. Bring to a simmer, then reduce the heat to low and simmer gently for 4–5 hours, regularly skimming any scum that rises to the surface.

5 Strain the stock through a fine-meshed sieve placed over a clean saucepan, discarding the solids. Simmer over medium heat for 30–40 minutes or until reduced to a sauce consistency. Strain again, leave to cool and use as required.

Jus is a concentrated stock that adds richness and depth of flavour to sauces. It will keep for up to 7 days in the fridge or up to 3 months in the freezer.

LAMB JUS

MAKES ABOUT 1 LITRE

3 kg lamb bones
1 tablespoon vegetable oil
2 onions, cut in half
2 carrots, diced
2 stalks celery, cut in half
1 leek, well washed and cut in half
2 sprigs thyme
2 bay leaves
1 bulb garlic, cut in half crossways
1 tablespoon tomato paste
6 roma tomatoes, chopped and seeded
1 cup (250 ml) white wine
1 litre chicken stock (see page 222)
1 litre veal jus (see page 224)
½ bunch tarragon

1 Preheat the oven to 180°C.

2 Place the lamb bones in a roasting tin and roast for 30–40 minutes or until golden brown, then remove and drain off the fat.

3 Heat the oil in a large stockpot over medium heat, add the onion, carrot, celery, leek, thyme, bay leaves and garlic and cook for 10 minutes or until golden brown.

4 Add the roasted lamb bones, tomato paste, chopped tomato, white wine, chicken stock, veal jus and 1 litre water and bring to a simmer. Cook for 2 hours, regularly skimming any scum that rises to the surface.

5 Remove the stockpot from the heat, add the tarragon and leave to stand for 15 minutes.

6 Strain the stock through a fine-meshed sieve placed over a clean saucepan, discarding the solids, then simmer over medium heat for 20–25 minutes or until reduced to a sauce consistency. Strain again, leave to cool and use as required.

BORDELAISE SAUCE

MAKES 300 ML

30 ml olive oil
100 g chicken wings, roughly chopped
  (ask your butcher to do this for you)
3 golden shallots, sliced
½ clove garlic, chopped
1 rasher bacon, chopped
1 bay leaf
1 cup (250 ml) red wine
300 ml veal jus (see page 224)

1 Heat the olive oil in a large saucepan until hot, then add the chicken wings and cook over medium heat for 5 minutes or until golden brown. Add the shallot, garlic, bacon and bay leaf and cook over low heat, stirring, for 2–3 minutes or until the shallots start to caramelise.

2 Deglaze the pan with the red wine, scraping all the sediment from the bottom of the pan, then simmer for another 3–4 minutes or until reduced by half. Add the veal jus and bring to the boil, then reduce the heat to low and simmer for 45 minutes, skimming away any scum from the surface.

3 Strain the sauce through a fine-meshed sieve placed over a clean saucepan and use as required.

MUSTARD SAUCE

MAKES 220 ML

200 ml chicken jus (see page 224)
1 teaspoon tarragon leaves, chopped
1 teaspoon Dijon mustard
1 teaspoon seeded mustard

1 Heat the chicken jus in a small saucepan over medium heat until hot. Add the tarragon and mustards and whisk to combine well, then use as required.

ACKNOWLEDGEMENTS

Thanks to:

All the wonderful staff at ARIA, in particular Simon Sandall, Ben Turner, Andrew Honeysett, Laura Baratto and Ben Russell.

My trusted suppliers, including Anthony, Anita and Vic Puharich from Vic's Premium Quality Meat, John and Bree Velluti from Velluti's – The Fruit and Veg Company and Jules Crocker from Joto Fresh Fish.

At Penguin, Julie Gibbs, Ingrid Ohlsson, Virginia Birch, Evi Oetomo, Alison Cowan, Nicole Abadee, Megan Pigott, Clio Kempster and Tracey Jarrett.

Photographer Chris Chen, stylist Michelle Noerianto and recipe tester Leanne Kitchen.

A special thanks to Peter Sullivan, Bruce Solomon, Ardleigh Matthews, Susan Sullivan and Sophie Landa for your ongoing support and last of all, but most importantly, my family Sarah, Harry, Amelia and Freddy.

We would like to thank the following for the generous loan of props and equipment for the photoshoot:

Aura by Tracie Ellis, Avanti, Bodum, Cuisinart, Global, Maxwell & Williams, Mud Australia, Robert Gordon Australia, Scanpan and Villeroy & Boch.

INDEX

LANTERN

Published by the Penguin Group
Penguin Group (Australia)
250 Camberwell Road, Camberwell, Victoria 3124, Australia
(a division of Pearson Australia Group Pty Ltd)
Penguin Group (USA) Inc.
375 Hudson Street, New York, New York 10014, USA
Penguin Group (Canada)
90 Eglinton Avenue East, Suite 700, Toronto, Canada ON M4P 2Y3
(a division of Pearson Penguin Canada Inc.)
Penguin Books Ltd
80 Strand, London WC2R 0RL England
Penguin Ireland
25 St Stephen's Green, Dublin 2, Ireland
(a division of Penguin Books Ltd)
Penguin Books India Pvt Ltd
11 Community Centre, Panchsheel Park, New Delhi – 110 017, India
Penguin Group (NZ)
67 Apollo Drive, Rosedale, North Shore 0632, New Zealand
(a division of Pearson New Zealand Ltd)
Penguin Books (South Africa) (Pty) Ltd
24 Sturdee Avenue, Rosebank, Johannesburg 2196, South Africa

Penguin Books Ltd, Registered Offices: 80 Strand, London, WC2R 0RL, England

First published by Penguin Group (Australia), 2011

10 9 8 7 6 5 4 3 2 1

Designed by Evi O. © Penguin Group (Australia)
Photography by Chris Chen
Styling by Michelle Noerianto
Typeset in Trade Gothic by Post Pre-Press Group, Brisbane, Queensland
Colour reproduction by Splitting Image Colour Studio Pty Ltd, Clayton, Victoria
Printed and bound in China by 1010 Printing International Limited

National Library of Australia
Cataloguing-in-Publication data:

Moran, Matt.
Dinner at Matt's / Matt Moran; with photography by Chris Chen.

9781921382734 (hbk.)
Includes index.

Cooking, Australian.
Chen, Chris.

641.5994

penguin.com.au/lantern